AIRLIFE'S AIR

BOEING
747-400

BOEING 747-400

Peter Gilchrist

Airlife
England

First published in the UK in 1998
by Airlife Publishng Ltd

British Library Cataloguing-in-Publication Data
   A catalogue record for this book
   is available from the British Library

ISBN 1 85310 933 9

Printed in Singapore by Kyodo Printing Co (S'pore) Pte Ltd..

Airlife Publishing Ltd
101 Longden Road, Shrewsbury, SY3 9EB, England

COVER: The baseline passenger 747-400: Virgin Atlantic's G-VFAB *Lady Penelope*.
Rob Holder

PREVIOUS PAGE: British Airways' short-lived intermediate colour scheme seen on
747-436 G-BNLN *City of Portsmouth* taking-off from Heathrow. *Rob Holder*

BELOW: Night at Narita: All Nippon 747-481 JA8098 was delivered to the airline in
August 1991. It is seen at Tokyo's Narita airport in March 1993. *Robbie Shaw*

CONTENTS

INTRODUCTION

There are certain moments in life that you seem to remember with almost perfect clarity: one such was my first close-up view of a Boeing 747, as it slowly taxied into sight from behind the sheds and offices of what was then the new cargo handling area on the south side of Heathrow Airport.

I was fortunate enough to be a guest of Pan American on that damp January morning in 1970 — initially to watch the arrival of the first proving flight to London, and later to join a brief demonstration ride in the aircraft — along with a group of other journalists and about 200 representatives of the travel trade. Surrounded as we were by two-storey buildings, it was impossible to see the actual approach and touch-down of the 747, and a tantalising brief glimpse of it in full reverse thrust on the distant, puddle-washed runway, did little to prepare anyone for the sheer majestic size of the aircraft.

Having been brought up in the 'big-jet' era of 707s, DC-8s and VC10s, we were all amazed by the sight of the cockpit and tail assembly of the new Boeing, making stately progress along the parallel taxyway and first becoming visible *above* the surrounding buildings. As the aircraft finally arrived on the pan, everyone was transfixed by the enormity of it all — we were aware that something in the industry had changed forever, although none of us could quite believe it.

Since that memorable day, wide-bodied aircraft have

BELOW: The visual charcteristics of the 747-400 series are obvious in this view of 747-437 Combi VT-ESO *Khajurahi* landing at Heathrow in April 1997: the winglets at the ends of the extended wings, stretched upper deck (as the -300). What is not visible are the revolutionary changes to the 747 'Classic' flightdeck that reduced the three-man crew to two. VT-ESO was delivered to Air India in December 1993 — and is currently one of six 400 series aircraft with the airline. *G. M. Harber*

overwhelmed our key passenger routes so completely, that the few remaining 707s and DC-8s now begin to look like the chihuahuas of the air travel business. I have taken a close interest in all aspects of 747 development, and have been lucky enough to fly on most major variants of the aircraft — both as a passenger, and as an observer on the flightdeck. I have watched many crews at work, and have always been impressed by their total confidence in the aircraft, its systems and its avionics: it was a superb design when it began its commercial life in the early 1970s, and has been steadily improved since then.

In its latest 400-series manifestation, Boeing's flagship airliner is even more remarkable. The original 1970s aircraft was certificated for a 710,000lb (322,050kg) maximum take-off weight — which, in its day, was nearly twice the weight of any commercial jet. Late 1990s versions are now routinely operating at 875,000lb (396,890kg) — a 165,000lb (74,845kg) development increase, which is roughly equivalent to the original model taking-off with a fully loaded Boeing 737 on its back!

Most of the original engineering team that created this amazing aircraft have long since departed, but the torch has now been passed to a new generation, and their blend of old and modern technologies has conjured up a masterpiece which will probably outlive us all. There is a demand for even more range and passenger capacity, and sooner or later the 747 will be stretched or changed to meet these new airline requirements—although the proposed -500 and -600 developments, announced so emphatically in 1996, have been shelved for the moment. These and several other ideas have already been explored, but none of them has attracted the essential launch orders in sufficient quantities.

In the meantime, 747-400s continue to sell in considerable numbers, and with the takeover by Boeing of McDonnell Douglas in August 1997, the company is set to dominate the airliner market in the future as it has done in the recent past. Certainly Boeing's most famous product, and the production line at Boeing's giant assembly building at Everett, near Seattle in Washington State, look as though they will remain active well into the next century.

ABOVE: British Airways G-BNLZ *City of Perth* in intermediate colour scheme landing at Heathrow. *Rob Holder*

RIGHT: This photograph, with the image compressed by the telephoto lens, nevertheless gives a good indication of the feeling of size, height and power of the aircraft which I saw for the first time in January 1970. Some 27 years after that event, t his is F-GISE, one of Air France's five 747-400 Combis; it was delivered to the airline in May 1993 and is seen here in March 1997 in Beijing. *Robbie Shaw*

ACKNOWLEDGEMENTS

Every book is a co-operative venture, and this one is certainly no exception. Unusually tight time constraints made it difficult to research such a complex aeroplane and still complete all the normal tasks of a lone author: without the help of a number of trusted friends, it would have been quite impossible. Simon Forty has worked tirelessly to produce a substantial amount of the final text, and really deserves to be credited on the cover as co-author.

Airline pilots Captain Bob Warnock and Captain Dave Peet have patiently provided advice and guidance on some of the more detailed aspects of flying an aircraft with digital systems and electronic instrumentation, helping to make a complicated subject less incomprehensible! Dr Hugh Newell, Dave Charles, Hans Jakobsson and Gabor Kerekes have all responded magnificently to requests for help with individual aspects of the research; and many of the illustrations and photographs have come from fine personal collections of Geoff Harber, Bob Holder, Hugh Newell, Leo Marriott, Robbie Shaw, Gerry Manning, Günter Endres and, of course, Boeing itself, whose assistance is acknowledged gratefully.

Finally my thanks are due to John Roach and Tony Eastwood for their considerable help with the 747-400 production list: this information was extracted and updated from their database for the excellent *Jet Airliner Production List* — which includes a comprehensive service history of each airframe, and is published by The Aviation Hobby Shop, West Drayton, Middlesex.

Peter Gilchrist
Farnham, March 1998

1 EVOLUTION

INTRODUCTION

The Boeing 747-400 is the latest development of the most remarkable aircraft in modern commercial history: the original 'Jumbo Jet', which allowed a quantum leap forward in terms of passenger numbers carried over intercontinental distances. From the first the 747 was an aircraft that could only be described in superlatives: it was bigger, flew farther and carried more passengers than any other commercial aircraft — its stablemate, the 707, for example, the first successful jet airliner, first flew in 1958 carrying up to 179 passengers; the first 747 flew 12 years later in 1969 and could carry over 400. Today, the 747's size and load-carrying differentials may have been eroded in comparison with more modern aircraft, but there's still only one Jumbo Jet.

The latest model of Boeing's remarkable wide-body is the 747-400, which usually carries around 420 passengers, although its maximum permissable seating is a staggering 660. It can carry its 420 passengers for about 8,300 miles (13,300km): in comparison, the latest Airbus, the 340, usually carries around 300 people for about 7,000 (11,200km). The 747-400 is also a thoroughly modern aircraft, a substantial development of its predecessors, with improvements that bely its aging antecedents. It has a two-pilot digital EFIS flightdeck, a new interior, and is powered by stronger, more efficient engines. With its huge capacity, extended range and improved fuel efficiency, Boeing boasts that the 747-400 offers the lowest operating costs per seat/km of any commercial jetliner.

It does so at a cost: Boeing's published figures show the relative prices for its aircraft — and those of recent acquisition McDonnell Douglas:

Aircraft Type	Cost in $ millions
717-200	30.5-34.5
737-300	38.5-44.5
747-400	158.5-176.5
757-300	69.0-76.0
767-300ER	97.5-108.5
777-200IGW	136.0-155.0
MD-80	41.5-48.5
MD-90	47.5-55.0
MD-11	129.0-144.0

The 747-400 comes in four forms: a basic passenger version, a combi — carrying passengers forward and cargo aft on the main deck — a domestic version and as a freighter which can transport more cargo farther than any other commercial jet freighter. It also has the lowest operating cost per ton-mile of all freighters, with fuel burn per pound of payload more than 15 percent better than the 747-200 Freighter, which ceased production in 1991. But this is not necessarily the final word in the

BELOW: Boeing 747 'prototype' N7470, the first development 747 and the first aircraft to fly, emerges into the sunshine at Everett on its roll-out, 30 September 1968—just 30 months after the go ahead was given for the project. *Boeing*

amazing story of the Jumbo: Boeing has mooted two new models of the Boeing 747. At a press briefing at the Farnborough Air Show on 2 September 1996, the president of Boeing Commercial Airplane Group, Ron Woodward, said that Boeing has been working with more than a dozen airlines in preliminary design and configuration studies of two new 747s, combining the benefits of the 747-400 with the systems and some of the interior features of the new 777. The 747-500X, was intended to be capable of carrying 462 passengers up to 10,000 miles with 10 tons-plus of extra cargo capacity. The 747-600X was planned to have seating for 548 passengers and a range of 8,900 miles (14,300km).

While recent thinking has moved Boeing to shelve these plans to develop derivatives of its other airliners — specifically the 757, 767 and 777 — it would be surprising if this were the end of the road in development terms for the 747. Perhaps, as Woodward went on to say at the same press briefing, there may be a need for an even larger aircraft in the future.

TOP: 747-100 series N9662 to the very original design: note three-window upper deck which at this time was used as a bar and passenger relaxation area. The term 'Classic' is now used to denote all three-crew non-digital aircraft. *Boeing*

ABOVE: Aerolineas Argentinas LV-LZD, an uprated 747-200B series 350-passenger version: note there are now normal passenger windows in the upper deck. *Boeing*

If so Boeing could meet that need with a larger derivative called the 747-700X. 'We could "re-body" the 747-600X with a wider fuselage, while retaining the existing wing, systems, engines, struts and landing gear,' he explained. 'The 747-700X would carry up to 650 passengers and have a design range equal to that of the 747-400.'

Only the future will see whether such behemoths will be carrying passengers in the 21st century, but if the spiralling increases seen in passenger numbers in the latter part of the 20th century continue, it seems likely that the requirement will be there.

HISTORY

It seems hard to believe that less than a century divides man's first powered flight and today's overcrowded skies. When, at Kitty Hawk, South Carolina on 17 December 1903, the Wright brothers did the impossible and defied gravity, they started a process of development that would see air transport become commonplace. Many people have contributed to this development, but at the start of the 21st century one name has come to dominate the market: Boeing.

The history of what has developed into the massive Boeing Commercial Airplane Group started only a few years after the Wright brothers' famous flight. In 1915 Seattle timberman William Boeing and his friend naval officer Conrad Westervelt decided they could build better aircraft than those around at the time: they went ahead and did so, producing the Model 1 (B & W). Fifty of the seaplane that was developed — the Model 5 — were ordered by the US Navy in 1917, and the Boeing Airplane Company (named thus on 26 April 1917) was on its way.

Since then, the history of Boeing has run alongside the history of aviation in the United States. The company moved from building fighters after World War I to bombers and commercial transports in the 1930s and 1940s. And while competi-

ABOVE: The 747SP is unique because it has double-slotted flaps rather than the triple-slotted flaps of all other 747 models. Note the lack of flap supports appearing from the back of the wing (compare back edge of wing with that in the photograph on page 13). *Boeing*

RIGHT: F-BPVR is a CF6-50E-powered 747-200 freighter with nose and side cargo doors; note lack of passenger windows and the Boeing certification registration number N1783B, temporarily allotted to the aircraft for flight test purposes. Just visible in the background is the snowy original profile of Mount St Helens, which would erupt so dramatically in 1991. *Boeing*

tors such as Douglas made more impression with its DC series, particularly in the sheer number of its aircraft that saw commercial use after the end of World War II in the form of the ubiquitous DC-3, Boeing got the hang of building big aircraft: its B-29 Superfortress weighed nearly 70,000lb empty (as compared to the 17,000lb (7,700kg) of the DC-3, the 33,000lb (15,000kg) of the B-29's predecessor, the B-17 Flying Fortress or the 37,000lb (16,800kg) of the British Lancaster) and the US Air Force would receive nearly 4,000 by the end of the war. The two most famous of these were *Enola Gay* and *Bock's Car*, the B-29s that dropped the first atomic bombs. Boeing also got the hang of maximising the lifespan of its aircraft in families — the B-17 spawned the Model 307 Stratoliner; the B-29 led to

the Model 367 — better known as the C-97 family of transports and tankers — and Model 377 Stratocruiser.

Following World War II, in 1954, Boeing developed the aircraft which would see the real start of the commercial jet age: the 707. While it may not have been the first jet airliner in service (that honour fell to the de Havilland DH106 Comet) the 707, derived from the programme to improve the Boeing Model 367, was destined to revolutionise air travel: its performance meant, quite simply, that all long-range commercial aviation in future would have to be jet-powered and pretty quickly so too would be the aircraft plying medium/short-range bulk passenger routes. The 707 would lead to a series of Boeing jets that would dominate the postwar commercial aviation market, selling in numbers unthought-of before the war. However, the revolution cost Boeing dear: $16 million in development costs were allocated to the Model 367, and even with sizeable military orders for the original KC-135 tanker, Boeing would take a long time to break even — it is said that it did not do so until 1,000 707s, KC-135s and 720s had been built.

The jets were substantially more expensive than piston-engined aircraft in unit cost to customer terms — a piston-engined Model 377 cost $1.5 million in 1948, a new 707-100 cost $4.8 million in 1958. These costs continued to escalate as did running and handling costs, but jet aircraft were phenomenally successful in increasing passenger numbers. Boeing was able to cater for these passengers in short/medium-haul terms with the 727 and 737, both of which sold in substantial numbers. However, it became obvious to Boeing that a huge leap was necessary to cope with increased passenger demand on long-range, particularly intercontinental, routes: that vision led to the 747.

THE 747

The mid-1960s was a good time to begin developing a large aircraft — as well the explosive increase in air-passenger traffic it was before the strictures of the fuel crisis and before the age of jet noise reduction requirements. Increasingly crowded skies and the availability of large-thrust engines added to the incentive for creating the giant 747. On top of this, Boeing — with its history of large aircraft — had a start on the design and technology of such an aircraft because the company had put in a serious bid for the contract for a gigantic military transport.

In 1963, the US Military Air Transport Service conducted an exercise called 'Big Lift', during which it moved the US Army's 2nd Armored Division from Texas to what was then West Germany. The move showed the world what the Pentagon had known for some time — the move of 15,300 men and their personal equipment a distance of some 5,600 miles was accomplished in straightforward manner by over 200 aircraft: but the heavy equipment of the tank division — ie the tanks! — had to be stored in situ, in depots vulnerable to enemy attack, because there was no aircraft in the USAF inventory capable of carrying that sort of load.

The operational requirement for the large transport aircraft that resulted was the CX-HLS. This saw three companies — Douglas, Boeing and eventual winners Lockheed — given $400,000 each to fund further studies for the airframe, and two engine manufacturers, General Electric and Pratt & Whitney, given funds for engine development. While Boeing would not end up building the resultant C-5 Galaxy, an aircraft that could carry twice as much as its nearest competitor nearly twice as far, and Pratt & Whitney would not provide the engines, both had learned much about the subject of massive

ABOVE LEFT: Called 'The Big Orange' by Braniff International, these spectacular 747SPs operated scheduled routes from Gatwick to the US mainland. The SP's fuselage is only just over 56m (184ft) long compared to the 70.66m (231ft) of the standard aircraft. *Boeing*

ABOVE: The inelegant suffix SUD — stretched upper deck — later became the 747-300, the only stretch of the 747; this fuselage was the basis for the 747-400. UTA — Union de Transport Aeriens — was eventually absorbed into Air France at the end of 1992. *Boeing*

aircraft structures. For Boeing, CX-HLS would lead directly to the 747; for Pratt & Whitney, the JT9D series engine — the lead powerplant on the 747.

Following the loss of the CX-HLS contract, Boeing looked very carefully at the market for large commercial aircraft and announced the Model 747 in April 1966. The launch customer was Pan American, who ordered 25. The rest, as they say, is history. By the time the first 747-400 set a new official weight record on 27 June 1988 by reaching an altitude of 2,000m at a gross weight of 892,450lb, the order book for the 747 stood at over 800: today it's at nearly 1,300 with 1,139 delivered. Of those delivered, over 400 are 747-400 series aircraft — more than any other individual model.

It is not intended that this book should provide a detailed history of the development and design of the initial 747: a later title in the 'Airlife's Airliners' series will look in detail at the 747-100 through to the 747-300. However, there is bound to be some slight overlap in the design, production and technical specification sections and this will be kept to a minimum. As a summary of the 747 achievements to date, one can do worse than examine excerpts from a press release issued in spring 1997 showing international recognition for the success of the design.

The press release was issued after the Boeing 747 design team had won the Francois-Xavier Bagnoud Aerospace Prize*:

'The four engineers who designed the Boeing 747 [Joseph Sutter, Kenneth F. Holtby, Everette Webb and Robert A. Davis], which has carried 1.8 billion people almost 25 billion miles, have won the third Francois-Xavier Bagnoud Aerospace Prize.

'In announcing the 1997 winners, Thomas C. Adamson, Jr., chair of the Aerospace Prize Board, said that the 747 — which rolled out of the factory in September 1968 and began commercial service in January 1970 — "brought striking reductions in air travel costs through its still unsurpassed combination of speed, range, and capacity . . . Truly, the world knows itself better now because of the reliable, capable Boeing 747 and its visionary developers." The 747 — the largest commercial airplane in the world with 6 million parts — has changed the face of aviation, relying on 1,101 domestic and international suppliers, with 79 percent of its sales outside the United States — nearly $98.3 billion in today's dollars. But perhaps its most poignant legacy is that the Boeing 747 has brought great quantities of people together for commerce, peace and relief, carrying enough passengers to equal one-fourth of the world's population.'

* The Francois-Xavier Bagnoud Aerospace Prize was established in 1992. The $250,000 aerospace prize is named in honour of Francois-Xavier Bagnoud, the youngest professional instrument flight rated pilot in Europe in the early 1980s of both airplanes and helicopters. Bagnoud died in a helicopter accident in Mali, Africa, in 1986, at the age of 24. Administered by the Aerospace Engineering department of the University of Michigan, Bagnoud's alma mater, it commemorates the bravery of someone who participated in more than 300 successful helicopter rescue missions in the Alps. The recipient of the first prize was William H. Pickering, who as head of the Jet Propulsion Lab in California was the guiding force behind the launching of the first US satellite. The US Apollo Program was awarded the second FXB prize for its lunar landings.

2 DESIGN

BACKGROUND TO THE 747-400

When Boeing engineers started work on the huge 747 project way back in the mid-1960s, all their market research had confirmed that the future for such a big airliner was likely to be fairly good — at least in the relatively short term. In the longer-term however — beyond a period of perhaps ten years or so — the prospects of a continuing future for passenger-carrying versions of the aircraft were much more doubtful. Supersonics, after all, were on the near horizon, and plainly this would be the direction that all long-haul commercial flying would take as soon as the technology became widely available. Big subsonic jets — at least in their prestige passenger-carrying role — would almost certainly be killed-off by the glamour of super-sonic competition, and most of these expensive aircraft would probably end their days being relegated to charter or cargo services. Seattle was so convinced by this gloomy vision of the future that the unique configuration of the 747 — with its cock-pit-section hoisted way above the main load space — was dictated solely by the long-term need to provide a large cargo-door in the nose, for straight-through containerised loading onto an uninterrupted main deck. All major elements of the 747 air-frame were therefore optimised for efficient cargo operations. By manufacturing large numbers of specialised freighters (and indeed by retro-fitting redundant passenger aircraft with nose-doors), it was hoped that the costly Everett production facilities could be kept going for several years beyond the magical age of supersonic passenger jets. To keep a foothold in both camps, a parallel team of Boeing designers was working flat-out on a Government-funded US supersonic transport (SST) programme — which was trying to find a successful formula for airliner to transport 250/300 people across the Atlantic at around Mach 2.7.

As we now know, a deeper analysis of the costs and technical risks involved, together with concerns for the environment, effectively put an end to the era of mass supersonic travel before it really got off the ground. The American decision not to participate, left the Anglo-French Concorde completely unchallenged in a relatively small, but highly prized, sector of the market. Large-capacity subsonic aircraft — undoubtedly led by the giant 747 — were later able to absorb a huge increase in both business and holiday travel, and to sustain this strong pattern of growth over a period of more than two decades. Much to the surprise of its early development team, the 747 not only remains at the forefront of passenger operations in the late-1990s, but the demand for new and updated models is possibly stronger now that it was for the original aircraft nearly 30 years ago.

During the first 20 years of its life, the 747 became an industry-standard among long-haul airliners: nothing could quite touch it for weight-lifting capability, seating-capacity or range. By the mid-1980s however, airline route structures had begun a process of development and change that would leave the 747 looking increasingly isolated and less attractive as a long-term investment. Despite a series of updates and model changes since its inception, the aircraft was beginning to show its age, and new orders had fallen to an all-time low of about 20 a year. Questions were being raised about the whole future of the Everett line, and the possibility of bringing 747 production to an end was openly discussed for the first time.

While all this was happening, countries around the Pacific rim had quietly created an enormously powerful economic region, and airlines operating in and through that area were growing at a tremendous pace. Lucrative business travel between city pairs such as Singapore/Los Angeles, Hong Kong/Vancouver, Tokyo/New York and Sydney/London was developing much faster than anyone had dared hope, and new routes were being opened up all the time to take advantage of near-boom conditions. Most of these transPacific routes — and indeed a growing number of highly desirable routes within the triangle formed by South America, Europe and Africa — were more than 5,500nm (10,000km) long, which often put them beyond the reach of an economical load with existing models of the 747. The aircraft itself was capable of these extreme ranges, but the weight of fuel needed to complete a journey of more than about 5,000nm (9,250km) imposed severe payload limitations especially when the departure originated in the overheated conditions of SE Asia. The airlines badly needed an aircraft that could handle these longer-range sectors without load restrictions — even against the strongest of winter headwinds.

Boeing had been working for some time on a long-range version of the existing 747-300. This proposal — announced by Seattle in 1984 as the 747-300A (Advanced) — retained the stretched upper-deck configuration of the original, but it was designed to have a greater wing span, more fuel capacity and more-powerful engines: its avionics, systems-architecture and conventional three-man cockpit were all changed in minor ways, but they were still basically inherited from existing models of the 747. Had it been built, this aircraft would certainly have been capable of crossing the Pacific with a sensible load, but most of the potential customers wanted a

ABOVE RIGHT: Celebrating the 20th anniversary of the first 747 roll-out (see page 10), on 30 September 1988 N7470 overflew Boeing's Everett, Kent and Renton factories in company with the first 747-400, N401PW and — by special arrangement — also flew over downtown Seattle where so many owe their livelihood to Boeing. *Boeing*

RIGHT: The big forward cargo door of the 747F will accept very long cargoes, but the floor to ceiling height beneath the cockpit is limited to 8ft (2.44m). This Lufthansa 200F is loading a 40ft (12.2m) long container in December 1974. *Lufthansa*

more radical update of the whole aircraft to bring it into line with modern thinking on systems-design and cockpit technology. During the first few months of 1985, several important carriers — including British Airways, Singapore Airlines, KLM, Cathay Pacific, Qantas, Lufthansa and Northwest Airlines — got together to form a special 747 consultative group, initially to discuss their common operational requirements, but later to go to Boeing and put collective pressure on the planning departments. Members of the group were already big operators of earlier 747s, and owned nearly 100 aircraft of every major variant between them: it therefore seemed more than reasonable that they should have their say when it came to studies of a replacement aircraft.

Boeing has always been good at listening to its customers. After a wide-ranging series of discussions — not only with the organised airline group, but also with many other potential buyers — the minimum-change philosophy represented by the 747-300A was abandoned completely. Several of the possible customers for a new 747 had already ordered, or were about to order, one or other of the (then) brand-new 'glass-cockpit' airliners (the Airbus A310, or Boeing's own 757 and 767 series), and it was clear from the benefits offered by these new technologies that the future lay in digital avionics and systems: they offered more on-board facilities; were far more flexible in operation, and were much cheaper to buy and maintain than the conventional 'clockwork' instruments on a

traditional 747. The customers were unanimous in their opinion that any new aircraft would need to remain commercially competitive for many years to come, and then retain a high residual value when it came to being sold-on to its second or third operator.

After considering all these issues, Boeing decided to accept the challenge and go for a complete nose-to-tail revision of the basic 747 design. It would take longer and cost a lot more than a simple range-increase for the 747-300, but all the engineers at Seattle were enthusiastic about the project, and it seemed to make good business sense to bring their flagship airliner into line with modern thinking. The resulting 747-400 was not only a spectacular engineering achievement, but it seemed to manage the almost impossible task of giving the majority of airlines virtually everything they wanted.

The basic airframe of the finished 747-400 (the empty aircraft, as it emerged from the factory) was actually much

ABOVE LEFT: The marketing image for the 747-400 showing a smart executive-style paint scheme. *Boeing*

BELOW LEFT: In reality the first 747-400 flew with only an approximation of that scheme. N401PW is seen here with Boeing's faithful F-86 Sabre chase plane alongside. Difficult to make-out is the trailing probe attached to the top of the fin. *Boeing*

BELOW: A Boeing-prepared drawing of the major airframe improvements that were incorporated into the 747-400. *Boeing*

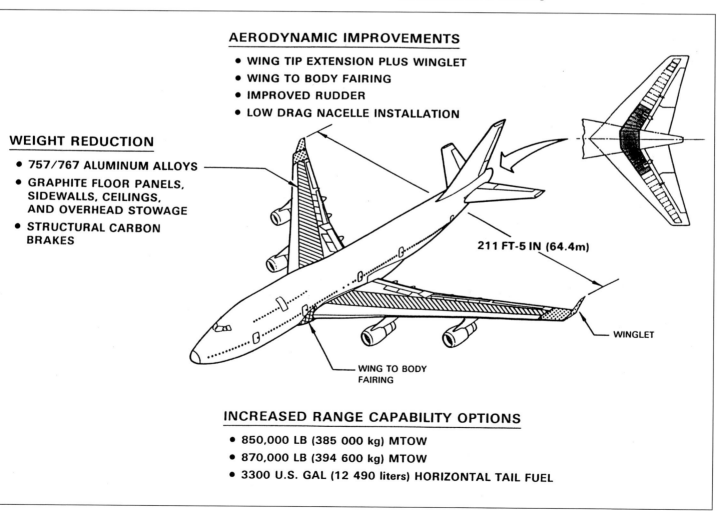

AERODYNAMIC IMPROVEMENTS
- **WING TIP EXTENSION PLUS WINGLET**
- **WING TO BODY FAIRING**
- **IMPROVED RUDDER**
- **LOW DRAG NACELLE INSTALLATION**

WEIGHT REDUCTION
- **757/767 ALUMINUM ALLOYS**
- **GRAPHITE FLOOR PANELS, SIDEWALLS, CEILINGS, AND OVERHEAD STOWAGE**
- **STRUCTURAL CARBON BRAKES**

211 FT-5 IN (64.4m)

WINGLET

WING TO BODY FAIRING

INCREASED RANGE CAPABILITY OPTIONS
- **850,000 LB (385 000 kg) MTOW**
- **870,000 LB (394 600 kg) MTOW**
- **3300 U.S. GAL (12 490 liters) HORIZONTAL TAIL FUEL**

lighter than the airframe of the similar 747-300, but its certificated gross take-off weight had gone up from 833,000lb (377,850kg) to 870,000lb (394,630kg): the maximum fuel capacity (with no optional tanks fitted) had been increased from the 747-300's 43,640 Imp gal (190,380 litres) to 44,640 Imp gal (202,940 litres). Typical fuel efficiency figures (in terms of fuel-burn per seat/km) of the new aircraft were between 7 percent and 11 percent better than those of the 747-300 — depending on the route flown. The net result of all these weight, capacity and efficiency changes represented a range increase of nearly 1,040nm (2,000km) over the 747-300, making it possible for the first time to fly a full load of 412 passengers over ranges well in excess of 7,000nm (13,000km).

By the time the 747-400 was launched in late 1985, nearly 700 conventional 747s had already been sold: orders were still trickling in for various models of the aircraft, but they were being received in very small numbers — mainly as top-ups to an existing fleet. Within just a few months of its launch, the strong demand for new 747s had completely revitalised the Everett factory — and incoming orders had switched from being additions to an established fleet, to large start-up orders or entire fleet renewals. The American carrier Northwest Airlines (formerly Northwest Orient) led the way with a launch order for 10 aircraft with Pratt & Whitney engines: these were quickly followed by an initial two with Rolls-Royce engines for Cathay Pacific, and six (later 10) for Lufthansa with General Electric engines. British Airways (16), KLM (6) and Singapore

Airlines (14) were next in the queue, closely followed by United Airlines (15), Air France (16) and Japan Airlines — initially with five firm orders, but later increased to 20.

Boeing would be the first to admit that the early popularity of the updated aircraft took everyone at Seattle by surprise, and the company was not really prepared for the huge increase in the number of orders. Carriers were almost falling over themselves to book early delivery positions, but the Everett line was stuck on a hopelessly inadequate production rate of less than two aircraft per month — with virtually no chance of doing anything to improve the situation for some time. Increasing the number of aircraft going through the factory requires thousands of extra staff, all of which have to be recruited, trained and supervised — often for months on end, and generally by the most experience factory hands. A number of really big items — such as the specialised wingplanks or massive undercarriage trucks — also have to be ordered many months in advance of their actually being needed in the final-assembly hall, which introduces similar problems of recruiting and training to each main supplier. These difficulties always generate a considerable time-lag between the decision to go for a higher production rate, and the ability to achieve the planned target. It finally took until the end of 1988 to raise production (of all 747 models) to four aircraft per month, and a further year to increase that total to five — by which time the continuing demand for the 400-series had forced Boeing to drop all the three-crew models from its product range.

On 10 September 1993 — almost 25 years to the week since the very first 747 had been rolled-out — Boeing's Everett production staff were able to celebrate the completion of the 1,000th 747 airframe (9V-SMU — a 747-412 for Singapore Airlines). By that time more than 270 400-series aircraft had been delivered to 27 different operators, and the firm-order backlog was approaching three figures. Press statements issued at the time of the 1,000th roll-out revealed that the total value of all 747 sales had reached the equivalent (adjusted for inflation) of $148.1 billion, of which more than $115 billion had been to non-US airlines: the programme accounted for nearly 80,000 full-time jobs, including 32,800 Boeing employees and more than 10,000 with overseas suppliers.

For a production programme that was not expected to survive for much more than about 10 years, the 747 has done remarkably well. Everett has already been building the aircraft for 30 years, and Boeing is currently laying the foundations for yet another major upgrade of the superbly designed basic structure: this will give the airlines even more range; allow them to carry more weight, and possibly include another 50/60 revenue-earning seats (depending on decisions yet to be made). Total sales of all past and present variants are now rapidly approaching the 1,300 mark, with the two-crew 400-series accounting for more than 550 of these.

RIGHT: Settled in to its test programme, the Pratt & Whitney-powered N401PW is seen high above Puget Sound near Seattle. At this time 20 customers had ordered 151 aircraft. *Boeing*

3 PRODUCTION

PRODUCTION

Boeing, as the biggest aircraft producer in the world, has had a lot of experience in building large, complicated aircraft. It has built up a huge and carefully controlled network of companies with whom it works, and many of these relationships and much of the organisation has been in place from the very beginning of the 747. With a capital involvement in design, tooling up and production facilities assessed as amounting to over $500 million in the late 1960s when the 747 was launched, it was obvious to Boeing that it would have to enter into profit-sharing partnerships with a host of manufacturers to spread the costs and risks. In the end over 50 percent of the cost of the early 747s was contracted out and a massive new final assembly plant was built on a 780-acre green field site at Paine Field, near Everett in Washington State. The world's largest building by volume cost $200 million. Here all the subassemblies and components are put together on a massive production line which has turned out over 1,000 747s in 15 versions from 747-100 to 747-400F.

The participating companies themselves also subcontract work, and so Boeing gets 747-400 major structures, subassemblies and nacelles from Northrop, who themselves have received fuselage frames for the upper decks from Daewoo Heavy Industries in Korea. Northrop Grumman, as the company is now called, has been a major partner in the 747 from the start, responsible for design and production of virtually the entire fuselage from just behind the flightdeck to the rear pressure bulkhead. Many, many others are involved from all over the world — undercarriage doors, for example, are made by Shorts of Belfast, and as far away as Japan Mitsubishi supplies inboard trailing edge and main landing-gear door actuators, Kawasaki the outboard trailing edge flap and Fuji the spoilers

RIGHT: The first completed 747-400 seen prior to its first flight during taxying trials at the Everett runway. *Boeing*

BELOW AND BELOW RIGHT: Two views of Everett — the more modern (BELOW) shows three paint shops in front of the huge main assembly building. On the other can be seen 22 747s, most of which are awaiting their engines during the troubles of the early 1970s. *Boeing*

and ailerons. These three are all members of Japan Aircraft Development, which also has a 20.8 percent share of the 777's structure, and produced 15 percent of the 767's airframe from 1978. JAD has approached Boeing for a similar workshare agreement on future 747 developments.

Such a massive organisation involving so many companies and such a large workforce is bound to go wrong at times. This, added to the fluctuations of market demands, can lead to serious manning difficulties and production problems have dogged the 747-400 from the start. Initially the problems were with certification of the aircraft with the three new engines on offer — the maiden flight of the P&W prototype was delayed by several weeks because of late component supplies and then integration of electronics, and similar problems affected the introduction of the Rolls-Royce and General Electric-powered versions. To compensate, the flight test schedule had to be accelerated and this clawed back some lost time but certification was four to eight weeks late on all three types.

On top of this, massive order increases across the Boeing range led to serious production line problems in late 1988 just as the 747-400 line was getting going. As new workers were recruited, so production was affected as their skill levels had to be raised — and delivery dates of the first 20 747-400s slipped at least a month. Compulsory overtime helped — until the workforce decided to go on strike because of the sheer slog of continued overtime. At the time it was assessed that the strike cost about 10 production slots: certainly the early customers of the 747-400 receive their aircraft late — most often the delay was limited to a month or two, but for some it was much longer: Qantas, for example, received its first 747-438 on 11 August 1989, some four months late, and UTA its first 400-4B3 on 22 September, five months late.

RIGHT: The bigger than expected carbon-skinned winglets and extended outer wing of the 747-400 give the aircraft its distinctive appearance. *Boeing*

BELOW: A giant forward fuselage subassembly being transported through the Everett factory on an overhead crane. *Boeing*

In more recent years, there have also been production problems — in 1995 and 1996 there were strikes of 90 and 60 days respectively and in September 1997 the aviation press reported increasing delays as Boeing struggled to put ambitious plans to increase production in place with inexperienced new workers, parts shortages and a stretched supplier base. In late 1997 the damage caused by these delays, which forced Boeing to shut down the Everett line for 20 days and delayed production of all Boeing aircraft, was put at $2.6 billion because of penalty clauses for late deliveries. Full production resumed in December but the damage had been done.

While the components of the aircraft are made by many partners, perhaps the most important of these are the world's big three engine manufacturers — Pratt & Whitney, General Electric and Rolls-Royce — all of whom produce engines for the 747-400.

PRATT & WHITNEY

Every three seconds, the Pratt & Whitney company sales information package says, somewhere around the globe, a P&W-powered aircraft takes-off or lands — an achievement which goes hand-in-hand with that of Boeing in the postwar civil aviation scene. The Pratt & Whitney Company was a machine-tool manufacturer in Hartford, Connecticut that was approached for backing in 1925 by Frederick Brant Rentschler, an Ohio graduate from Princeton. He wanted to build aircraft engines, and had learned from a high-ranking officer that the US Navy would be interested in an air-cooled engine in the 400 to 500hp range, but weighing no more than 650lb (295kg). Pratt & Whitney gave him backing, plant space and a respected name, and he repaid their faith with the first Pratt & Whitney engine — the Wasp TM, which was completed on Christmas

Eve 1925. It passed its qualification trials with flying colours, stunning the watchers with its performance. In 1926, little more than a year after Frederick Rentschler arrived, Pratt & Whitney booked its first contract: 200 Wasps for the US Navy.

Pratt & Whitney has had close associations with Boeing for many years. On 15 April 1952 a prototype Boeing B-52 Stratofortress took-off powered by eight Pratt & Whitney J57 turbojets, each producing 10,000lb (44.5kN) of thrust. Boeing would choose the J57 (called the JT3 for commercial purposes) to power its first prototype jet transport — the Model 367-80 which become the record-breaking 707.

If the turbojet was the dominant aircraft engine of the 1950s, more take-off thrust and better fuel consumption was required for the future and P&W's first production turbofan, the JT3D, made its first flight on a Boeing 707-120 on 22 June 1960. The new generation of wide-body jetliners required more than twice as much thrust, and this led to the JT9D — a distinct departure from earlier engine designs. A high bypass turbofan using a single-stage fan with a diameter nearly two-thirds the length of the engine, it was designed with emissions of both pollution and noise in mind and proved to be a winner. It was selected as lead-engine for the 747, and powered the aircraft for its first flight on 9 February 1969. In January of the following year, the JT9D entered commercial service on the inaugural

BELOW: The 75th 747 for Japanese Airlines was this -400 series aircraft seen nearing completion at Everett. From here it will go to the paint shop for its final finish before it begins its acceptance test programme. *Boeing*

New York-London flight of a Pan Am 747, the first of 60 airline operators worldwide to choose the engine. Indeed, the first 230 or so 747s all used P&W engines.

In the mid-1980s, Pratt & Whitney began development of PW4000 series turbofan — an all-new, third-generation 94in (2.4m) diameter turbofan, with take-off thrust ratings ranging from 50,000lb (222.5kN) to more than 62,000lb (275.8kN). The PW4084 powering the Boeing 777 made history on June 1995 by becoming the first aircraft/engine combination ever approved for 180-minute ETOPS (Extended-range Twin-engine Operations) right from the start. The 747-400 uses the PW4056, manufactured at Pratt & Whitney's 5.2-million square feet, 965-acre site at East Hartford. Recent airlines to choose Pratt & Whitney engines for 747-400s include Air China, who announced the choice on 7 August 1996 in a three-aircraft order which was valued, including spares, at approximately $100 million; Malaysia Airlines' $400 million order was for 40 PW4056 engines for its ten new 747-400s, as well as five spare engines worth $327 million — Malaysia had previously selected the PW4168 engine for its fleet of Airbus A330s and the PW4056 for its nine original 747-400s. The Taiwanese carrier China Airlines also selected PW4000 engines to power four firm orders and four options: total value of the engine order, including options, was approximately $270 million. Other long-term users are Korean, SIA and United.

GENERAL ELECTRIC

Despite P&W's early domination of the 747 engine market, it soon became clear that airlines wanted options and the first of these was the United States' other big engine manufacturer, General Electric. GE advertises itself as the world's leading manufacturer of military and commercial jet engines — and it is a massive manufacturer with a long history. As with Pratt and Whitney, GE began as a company in the 1920s — it was more than 75 years ago, that a 350hp turbosupercharged Liberty aircraft engine was fired up and earned GE its first aviation-related government contract. Since then, GE has scored many firsts, the most notable of which was building America's first jet engine: in 1941, the US Army picked GE's plant in Lynn, Massachusetts, to build a series of engines designed by Britain's Sir Frank Whittle. Six months later, in April 1942, GE's own engineers successfully ran the engine which launched America into the jet age.

The first engine to put the company on the postwar map was the J47, military demand for which was so great, including its use on the F-86 Sabre, that the Lynn plant could not keep up by itself. GE bought a second plant — at Lockland, Ohio, near Cincinnati — which opened on 28 February 1949 with the second J47 production line. Later, the plant would be known as Evendale and would grow to be much bigger than the Lynn plant. With the Korean War boosting demand, the J47 became the world's most produced gas turbine with more than 35,000 delivered by the end of the 1950s, and it became the first turbojet certified for commercial use by the Civil Aeronautics Administration.

However, the J47 was inadequate for the planned Century series of fighters, which would fly at more than twice the speed of sound. Again GE provided the solution — the variable-stator J79, more than 17,000 of which were built over 30 years, powering aircraft such as the F-104 Starfighter and F-4 Phantom II. On the Convair 880 airliner, the CJ805 derivative of the J79 engine marked GE's entry into the civil airline market and the addition of a fan to the rear of the CJ805 turbojet created the first turbofan for commercial service, used first on the Convair 990 in the early 1960s.

It was GE that won the race to power Lockheed's C-5 Galaxy, winner of the CX-HLS competition, with the TF39, the world's first high bypass turbofan. Building on that, GE entered the civil market in earnest in 1971 with the CF6 engine. This was first used on the DC-10 and it would go on to become the second choice of engine for the 747, available to customers in 1974.

Also in 1971, GE and Snecma of France became partners setting up CFM International as a 50/50 joint company to build engines based on French fan technology and the core of GE's F101 engine, which powers the B-1 bomber. CFM delivered its first engine in 1981 and since then the company has become increasingly successful: CFM56 (and CF6) engines will power airliners well into the next century.

Research and development on new engine lines continued, and another first is on the way: the GE90, designed to power future generations of airliners, is the world's largest, most powerful turbofan engine, with a fan 10ft (3.05m) in diameter and a thrust rating of 75,000lb-95,000lb (333.75kN-422.75kN). The GE90 was certified in February 1995, and entered into service on the Boeing 777. The CF6-80C2 57,000lb (253.65kN) thrust engine for the 747-400 was ordered initially by Lufthansa. Since then it has become the lead engine for the 747-400 with most airlines choosing it.

ROLLS-ROYCE

Rolls-Royce is the third of the world's great engine manufacturers to be involved with the 747-400. Formed by Henry Royce and Charles Rolls in 1906 to make motor cars, it quickly gained the reputation for making 'the best car in the world', with its Silver Ghost model. Aero engines were first produced in 1914, when Henry Royce designed the Eagle — his engine designs would go on to provide much of the total horsepower used in the air war by the Allies and the Eagle powered the first direct transatlantic flight as well as the first flight from England to Australia.

The late 1920s saw Rolls-Royce develop the 'R' engine to power the Supermarine S6 and S6B Schneider Trophy winners. This gave Rolls-Royce the technological base to develop the Merlin, which powered the Hawker Hurricane and Supermarine Spitfire in the Battle of Britain. Over 160,000 engines were built

ABOVE RIGHT: Excellent close-up of the wingtip winglet and outboard PW4056 of a Singapore Airlines 747-400 at Paris Charles de Gaulle. *Robbie Shaw*

RIGHT: Refuelling a Virgin Atlantic aircraft showing the underwing refuelling point; the 747 also carries a tail fuel tank. (See page 46.) *Robbie Shaw*

ABOVE: Close-up of the RB211-524H engines and underwing mountings on a British Airways 747-400. *Robbie Shaw*

ABOVE LEFT: Specially staged photo opportunity for the so-called 'first' delivery of British Airways' 747-400s on 26 July 1989. In fact the first BA 747-436 deliveries were formally made on 30 June 1989 (G-BNLA), 21 July 1989 (G-BNLC) and 31 July (G-BNLB). Note DC-3 and B-47 Stratojet to right of photograph. *Boeing*

BELOW LEFT: Another view of N401PW during taxi and braking trials — note the truck tucked under the port wingtip. *Boeing*

by Rolls-Royce, the Ford Motor Company in Britain and Packard in the United States for Lancasters, Mosquitos, P-51 Mustangs and a dozen other operational aircraft types.

During the war Rolls-Royce began development of the aero gas turbine engine, pioneered by Sir Frank Whittle, which entered squadron service in the Gloster Meteor in 1944 and a year later the Meteor. Rolls-Royce had the confidence immediately after the war to sideline piston engines and commit itself to the gas turbine, in which it had a technological lead. Many countries would replace their military aircraft with jets, either purchased from Rolls-Royce or built under licence. Then, in 1953, Rolls-Royce entered the civil aviation market with the Dart propjet in the Vickers Viscount.

In 1966, the British aero engine industry was consolidated when Rolls-Royce and Bristol Siddeley merged. Among many strengths Bristol Siddeley brought to the partnership were the unique Pegasus engine which powers the Harrier jump jet

and the Olympus 593, which powers Concorde, the world's only supersonic airliner. But it wasn't all a tale of success. In line with so much of Britain's postwar industry, there were labour and financial problems. The launch of the RB211 engine for the Lockheed L1011 TriStar led to such financial difficulties [See *Airlife's Airliners 2 Lockheed L1011 TriStar*] that Rolls-Royce had to be taken into ownership by the British Government in 1971. The subsequent success of the RB211 led to the company penetrating world airline markets, something which would lead to Rolls-Royce being returned to the private sector in 1987. Since then Rolls-Royce has extended its presence in aero propulsion with the acquisition in 1995 of the Allison Engine Company in the United States.

Rolls-Royce first became involved in the 747 programme in 1977, when the RB211-524B of 50,000lb (222.5kN) thrust was a used to power a new batch of British Airways 747-236s: since that time a number of other airlines have selected the British engine. The new 747-400 models are all powered by either the 58,000lb (258.1kN) thrust RB211-524G or the 60,000lb (267kN) -524H. As part of its continuous product improvement strategy, Rolls-Royce has now certified the latest models of these engines with the advanced Trent 700 high pressure core. This application of Trent technology enables the upgraded -524G/H-T to offer airlines the lowest fuel burn and lowest maintenance costs for the 747-400. It is said to give operators a 2 percent improvement in fuel consumption. It also gives an 800lb (364kg) weight saving per aircraft, and improves the engine's environmental impact, comfortably meeting all current and planned legislation on emissions. Certificated in 1997, this system has gained immediate interest: for example, on 19 August 1997 Cathay Pacific, the first airline to select Rolls-Royce engines for its 747-400s, took its first two aircraft. They were powered by -524Gs; thereafter the aircraft were equipped with -524Hs. Cathay has announced that it will convert all its 747-400 engines to the improved G/H-T standard — the first customer for which was South African Airways. Other Rolls-Royce-engined 747-400 users are British Airways, Qantas and Air New Zealand, all of which opted for the -524G.

ENGINE CHOICE

The first 747-400, N401PW, which later became N661US for Northwest, was powered by Pratt & Whitney engines, but it would be the General Electric CF6 that would become the lead engine for the type. The choice of engines has allowed airlines a variety of options — for example, Lufthansa chose CF6s to give commonality with its A300-600s and Malaysia chose PW4056 engines having selected the PW4168 engine for its fleet of Airbus A330s. Those that chose Rolls-Royce may have been impressed by the company's lead in wide-chord fan blades which are less vulnerable to air strike damage and are lighter.

A listing of engine choice by customer airlines is given below. However, it's worth noting that some fleets use more than one type of engine, often because of acquisition or leasing.

Air Canada	PW4056
Air China	PW4056
Air France	CF6-80
Air New Zealand	RB211-524/CF6-80
All Nippon Airways	CF6-80
Asiana Airlines	CF6-80
Atlas Air	CF6-80
British Airways	RB211-524
Brunei Government	CF6-80
Cargolux Airlines	CF6-80/RB211-524
Cathay Pacific Airways	RB211-524
China Airlines	PW4056
EVA Air	CF6-80
Garuda Indonesia Airways	CF6-80
Japan Airlines	CF6-80
KLM – Royal Dutch Airlines	CF6-80
Korean Air Lines	PW4056
Kuwait Airways	CF6-80
Lufthansa German Airlines	CF6-80
Malaysia Airlines	CF6-80

ABOVE: Artist's representation of the 747-400 Combi. *Boeing*

LEFT: Take-off from the puddle-washed runway at Everett of the first 747-400F dedicated cargo aircraft on 4 May 1993, carrying test registration N6005C. Due for Air France as F-GIUA, it was not taken up by that airline which changed its order in favour of Combis. After certification flying the aircraft was stored in Arizona for nearly two years before delivery to Cargolux as LX-ICV on 13 September 1995. *Boeing*

Northwest	PW4056
Philippine Airlines	CF6-80
Qantas	RB211-524
Singapore Airlines	PW4056
South African Airways	RB211-524
Thai Airways International	CF6-80
United Airlines	PW4056
UTA	CF6-80

747-400 PRODUCTION

By the time the 747-400 was launched, the sales figures for all Jumbo Jets had reached nearly 700; but the pace of orders was dwindling and the Everett line was down to two a month in 1984/85. The 747-400 family would kick start the programme to such an extent that of the 450 orders for the 747 received in the next five years, fewer than 100 were for earlier types. By May 1990, when Rolls-Royce's RB211-524H was added to the engine types certificated on the aircraft, only the -400 was being sold and later that year the 747-400F launch saw another rash of orders. A full list of 747-400 unit production is given in Chapter 7, the annual figures are:

1988	7
1989	40
1990	62
1991	64
1992	60
1993	57
1994	39
1995	22
1996	24
1997	39

4 TECHNICAL SPECIFICATION

Overall Dimensions	Imperial	Metric
Wing span	211ft 0in	64.03m
Wing span (747-400D)	195ft 8in	59.64m
Chord (at root)	54ft 4in	16.56m
Chord (at tip)	13ft 4in	4.06m
Tailplane span	72ft 9in	22.02m
Overall length	231ft 9in	70.07m
Fuselage length	225ft 2in	68.06m
Overall height	64ft 3in	19.06m
Wheelbase	84ft 0in	25.06m
Track	36ft 9in	11.00m
Turn Radius	140ft 4in	42.08m

Wing Characteristics		
Area	5,650sq ft	525.45sq m
Area (747-400D)	5,500sq ft	511.02sq m
Sweep (quarter chord)	37.5°	
Aspect ratio	7.0	
Angle of incidence	2°	

Internal dimensions		
Main deck length	187ft 0in	57.00m
Max width	20ft 1in	6.13m
Max height	8ft 4in	2.54m
Cabin volume	27,860cu ft	789cu m
Floor area	3,529sq ft	328sq m

Usable fuel	USgal	Ltr	Kg
Centre wing tank	17,153	64,973	52,162
Inner wing (tanks 2 and 3)	25,076	94,984	76,256
Outer wing (tanks 1 and 4)	8,879	33,932	27,242
Reserve tanks (outer wing)	2,642	10,008	8,035
Tailplane (stabiliser) tank	3,298	12,492	10,029
Fuselage tanks (optional)	1,720	6,511	5,227
Totals	58,768	229,900	178,951

WEIGHT AND PERFORMANCE SURVEY

DOM — Dry Operating Mass (Basic Operating Weight)

This is the basic weight of the aircraft, furnished, equipped and crewed for normal flight operations, but excluding the weight of usable fuel and payload. Typical DOM values for 747-400 variants (based on 870,000lb gross weight):

Basic passenger model	403,486lb	182,020kg
747-400 Combi	406,184lb	184,244kg
747-400D	392,909lb	178,222kg
747-400F	364,889lb	165,513kg

Zero Fuel Mass (Zero Fuel Weight)

This is the DOM of the airframe, plus the weight of the entire payload: the margin between ZFM and MTOM (see below) will tell the pilot how much fuel he can carry for that sector. Maximum ZFM values for 747-400 variants (based on 870,000lb gross weight):

Basic passenger model	535,000lb	242,670kg
747-400 Combi	565,000lb	256,227kg

	Imperial	Metric
747-400D	535,000lb	242,670kg
747-400F	610,000lb	276,635kg

MTOM — Max Take-Off Mass (Max Take-Off Weight)

Determined by structural and aerodynamic testing, the MTOM is certificated by appropriate regulatory bodies, and must not be exceeded at any time. Certificated MTOM values for all 747-400 variants (plus available options) are:

All early models	800,000lb	362,800kg
With tail-fuel option	850,000lb	385,475kg
Plus structural mods	870,000lb	394,545kg
Plus extra strengthening	875,000lb	396,812kg

Taxying Mass (Ramp Weight)

The MTOM is applicable at the start of the take-off roll. The TM represents an allowance for the fuel used to taxi from the airport gate to the runway. All models add a maximum of 3,000lb (1,360kg) to the MTOM figures.

Typical field length for take-off at 870,000lb (394,545kg)

ISA sea level	10,560ft	3,220m
ISA +20°C sea level	11,480ft	3,500m
ISA at 5,000ft (1,525m)	14,432ft	4,400m

Max Landing Mass (Max Landing Weight)

The certificated Max Landing Mass of each airframe is dictated by the optional strengthening of wing centre-section and undercarriage structures.

Early basic aircraft	574,000lb	260,309kg
Upgrade option 1	630,000lb	285,763kg
Upgrade option 2	652,000lb	295,760kg

Typical landing distance at 652,000lb (295,760kg)

ISA sea level	6,986ft	2,130m
ISA +20°C sea level	6,986ft	2,130m
ISA at 5,000ft (1,525m)	7,905ft	2,410m

Typical Speed, Altitude and Range Performance

Initial cruise: 34,000ft (10,200m) after 800,000lb (362,800kg) T/O
    33,000ft (10,065m) after 850,000lb (385,475kg) T/O
    32,000ft (9,760m) after 870,000lb (394,545kg) T/O
Max cruise altitude: 45,000ft (13,725m) after burning off fuel
Max cruise speed: 507kt at 35,000ft (10,675m)
Long-range cruise speed: 490kt at 35,000ft (12,250m)
Take-off rotation speed: 185kt (varies with weight)
Landing approach target speed: 152kt (varies with weight)
Normal operating Mach: 0.85 (cruise)
Max operating Mach: 0.92 (max cruise)

Range:	st miles	nm	km
full payload	8,406	7,300	13,528
full fuel	9,673	8,400	15,569

RIGHT: British Airways 747-436 G-BNLD *City of Belfast* showing off the size of the extended wing and the flap extension. *Robbie Shaw*

A NEW APPROACH TO THE 747

When the first of the new 747-400s emerged from the Everett factory, its complete re-design put it years ahead of the originally planned 'Advanced' version of the 747-300. The use of a new generation of structural alloys; new carbon brake units; new avionics, and a futuristic two-man flightdeck with fully automated systems, completely transformed the qualities of this icon of modern air travel. It had virtually become a brand-new aircraft, although in reality it remained a longer ranging, more capable version of an old friend — much easier to operate and look after, yet retaining all the curious charm of earlier members of the family.

THE WING

The most obvious external change from the 747-300 was the 'new' wing, which had been given more basic span and substantial, upturned winglets. This was actually the 10th time the original 747 wing had been re-designed, but all the earlier changes (with the exception of a much simpler flap configuration on the 747SP) had concentrated on revisions of the internal structure, and were therefore impossible to see from the outside. Had the engineers and aerodynamicists been given a completely free hand with the 747-400 project, they would probably have chosen a much bigger increase in basic span, rather than tackle the difficult aerodynamic issues raised by winglets. This particular aspect of the design, however, was dictated rather more by the dimensions of existing airport ramp areas and hangar doors, than it was by the need for idealised airflow

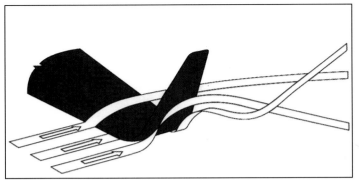

ABOVE: Drawing showing the theoretical straightening effect the winglet has on the vortex being generated by any wingtip. *Boeing*

BELOW: Qantas Rolls-Royce-powered VH-OJA *City of Canberra* shows to advantage the re-profiled wing/body fairing of the 747-400. *Leo Marriott*

ABOVE RIGHT: A Korean Air Lines 747-400 turns off the runway at Everett: note the way the wing bends downwards at the tips with the weight of fuel on-board. *Boeing*

BELOW RIGHT: 747-400 wing aerodynamic changes showing the six-foot (1.8m) tip extension and winglet. *Boeing*

solutions. The adoption of winglets was a necessary compromise: they provided a noticeable cost benefit from the reduction in drag during cruising flight, but avoided the problems of manoeuvring a significantly larger aircraft through a crowded airport. As part of the general aerodynamic update, the big wing/body fairing was completely re-profiled.

Increasing the span by stretching outwards from the existing wing-root would have provided a much bigger increase

WING SPAN: 211 FT 5 IN. (64.4m) NO FUEL
213 FT 0 IN. (64.9m) FULLY FUELED

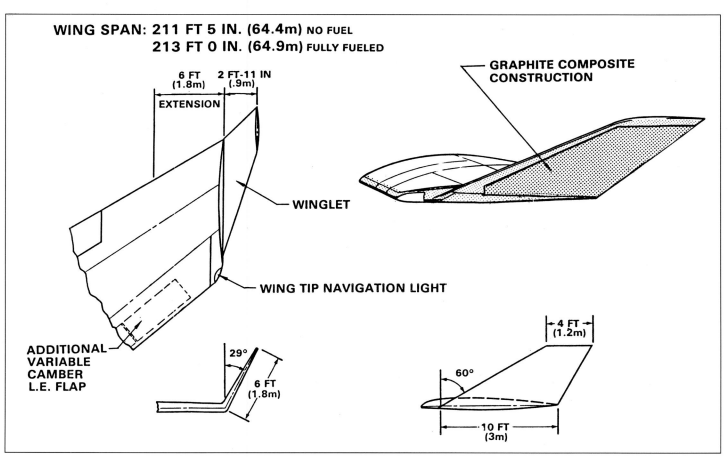

6 FT (1.8m)

2 FT-11 IN (.9m)

EXTENSION

GRAPHITE COMPOSITE CONSTRUCTION

WINGLET

WING TIP NAVIGATION LIGHT

ADDITIONAL VARIABLE CAMBER L.E. FLAP

29°

6 FT (1.8m)

4 FT (1.2m)

60°

10 FT (3m)

in available fuel-tank space, but it would also have been difficult to achieve technically, and would certainly have resulted in a much heavier and more expensive aircraft. Instead, the new 747-400 had an extra 6ft (1.83m) added to the outer wing panels on both sides, and the winglets were attached outboard of that. The winglet configuration developed for the aircraft was sharply swept back, and canted out from the vertical by 29° which means that the winglets themselves add an increasing amount to the span as they filled with fuel. With all the wing-tanks empty the structural span is 211ft 5in (64.46m), but when the tanks contain their full load of 245,800lb (111,500kg) of fuel, the outer wing bends slightly downwards under the weight, forcing the tip of the winglets to swing out to a total span of 213ft (64.92m). The longer basic span of the wing has allowed the inclusion of one additional section (each side) of Boeing's uniquely designed, variable-camber, leading-edge flap. All other flight controls, including the high and low speed ailerons, the spoilers and lift-dumpers, and the triple-slotted trailing-edge flaps, remain unchanged both in form and function from all earlier 747s. The 747-400 wing is an all-metal structure out to the end of the tip extension, but the winglets are made of composite materials and braced with metal spars.

Despite its 17ft (5.2m) span increase, the 747-400 wing is much lighter than the wing of the 747-300. This was achieved by using large quantities of the new 2000 and 7000-series alloys in its construction. These materials were specially commissioned by Boeing during the early stages of the 757 and 767 programmes, and had subsequently proved to be highly successful in both aircraft. Most of their great strength is gained from much more accurate control of the original alloying elements (copper in the 2000-series, and zinc for the 7000-series) during the complex manufacturing process of the raw-materials. These advanced alloys are anything up to 13 percent stronger than traditional aircraft materials, and have demonstrated the same properties of fatigue and corrosion resistance. Although they are fractionally lighter in themselves than familiar alloys, their increased stiffness has allowed the gauge of metal used in most components of the structure to be reduced. This had a dramatic effect on the weight of the 747's massive wing torsion-box, and finally in a saving of 5,500lb (2,500kg) per aircraft. At one stage in the 747-400 design Boeing even considered using some of the 8000-series (aluminium-lithium) materials: these would certainly have saved even more weight than the present alloys, but Al-Lith materials are difficult and expensive to produce, and in the end they simply proved too costly for the benefits they were expected to provide.

THE ENGINES

All three of the major Western powerplant manufacturers (Pratt & Whitney, General Electric and Rolls-Royce) have traditionally supplied engines for most models of the 747, and the whole aircraft programme continues to benefit from this intense competition. Many years of day-to-day operational experience has developed some of the most reliable powerplants the world has ever seen, with in-flight shut-down and unscheduled-removal rates that previous generations of engineers could only dream about.

The first three 747-400s were all powered by different engines. The Pratt & Whitney PW4000 series was developed as a follow-on replacement for the popular JT9D — the engine that powered the first ever 747, and all subsequent production aircraft until the General Electric CF6 joined the programme in the late summer of 1975. The new PW4000 series drew on much of the technology and construction techniques first used on the PW2037 (an optional powerplant on the Boeing 757). At the time of its introduction, much was made of the PW4000's 50 percent reduction in parts count compared with the latest version of the JT9D, but most of these 'parts' consisted of various fixing devices (nuts, washers, locking tabs, etc), which had largely been replaced on the new engine by welded subassemblies. Having said that, these new design techniques certainly made the difficult task of breaking down an engine, and then re-assembling it, very much easier, and this helped to reduce the overall maintenance costs by up to 25 percent. The specific engine selected for the 747-400 was the PW4056, which had a nominal thrust of 56,000lb/249.2kN (hence the 56 in the manufacturers designation). At the start of its service life, Pratt & Whitney was confident enough in the tested performance of the engine to give prospective customers a guaranteed specific fuel consumption figure that was 7 percent better than the latest standard JT9D-7R4: the eventual target figure — after a year or so of operational experience with various control settings — was no less than 11 percent. At 1987 fuel prices, and with an average utilisation of 10-11 hours per day, even the lower guaranteed figure would have yielded savings of well over $1 million per aircraft per year. The very first 747-400 (N401PW — later to be re-registered N661US for Northwest Airlines) was powered by the PW4056, and the engine has subsequently been selected by a number of other important carriers, including United, Korean, Singapore, Malaysia and China Airlines. Current (1998) engines in the series have been developed to generate nearly 60,000lb (267kN) of thrust.

The General Electric powerplant for the new 747 was the CF6-80C2 — which was initially developed from the CF6-80A1 to meet the high-thrust requirements of the big Airbus A300-600 and Boeing 767 twins. The -80C2 was fitted with a 93in diameter fan and a 4-stage low-pressure compressor (compared with the 86.4in (2.2m) fan and 3-stage compressor of the earlier CF6-80A1), and in this form it was capable of reaching thrust levels of up to 64,000lb (284.8kN). The model first used on the 747-400 was the CF6-80C2-B1F, which was slightly de-rated to a take-off thrust of 57,900lb (257.7kN). The first GE-powered 747-400s were ordered by Lufthansa, but the engine

RIGHT: Cutaways of the P&W 4000 series (TOP), GE CF6-80C2 (CENTRE) and RB211-524H (BELOW) turbofans showing an interesting comparison between the three-shaft layout of the British and two-shaft layout of the American engines. Of particular interest is lack of snubbers on the outer section of the wider-chord Rolls-Royce fan blades. The CF6 is shown in its nacelle: the yellow material around the fan blades is the multi-layered Kevlar containment shroud to stop broken fan blades from causing damage to the main structure of the aircraft. *Pratt and Whitney; General Electric; Rolls-Royce all via Leo Marriott*

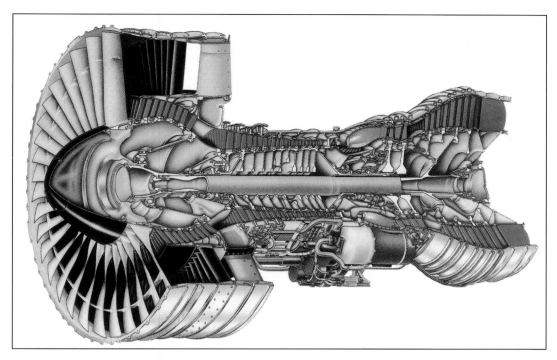

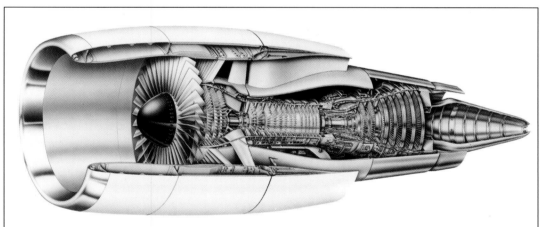

has since been specified by most of the big far-eastern carriers, including Japan Airlines, All Nippon Airways, Thai Airways International, Philippine Airlines and Asiana: the sheer quantity of aircraft operated by these airlines has effectively resulted in the CF6 becoming the lead engine on 747-400s. The latest versions of the engine are designed to meet much tougher emission-control standards than the original: they are also more fuel efficient, and now develop thrusts in the order of 61,000lb (271.5kN).

The modular engineering and assembly techniques used in the three-shaft Rolls-Royce RB211 gave the powerplant a great deal of flexibility in its basic design. The variants offered for the 747-400 were the 58,500lb (260.3kN) thrust RB211-524G, and the 60,000lb (267kN) thrust RB211-524H: these engines were more or less identical in their mechanical elements, but their control systems were slightly different. RB211s are assembled in seven individual sections (or modules), all of which can be removed from the wing and replaced or serviced separately. Each of the modules has been progressively improved over the last 20 years or so, which has allowed

LEFT: RB211-524G/H on the wing of a Qantas 747-400, showing the maintenance cowls open. *Rolls-Royce via Leo Marriott*

BELOW LEFT: CF6-80C2 publicity photograph highlighting the size and number of titanium fan blades. *General Electric via Leo Marriott*

BELOW: PW4000 series engine mounted in a test cell; note complexity of wiring and instrumentation between engine and control rig. *Pratt & Whitney via Leo Marriott*

many airlines to convert existing engines to a later standard — simply by buying and fitting the new module.

The RB211-524G/H used on the 747-400 has 24 wide-chord, hollow fan blades, which make the entire fan-assembly very light in relation to its thrust capability. Advanced blade design techniques have enabled Rolls-Royce to eliminate the mid-span anti-vibration snubbers which are carried by most engines in this class: this new configuration allows the fan to pump slightly more air for a given diameter, and it helps protect the core of the engine from bird-strike damage because a carcass that tries to go through the centre of the disc can now be thrown outwards by centrifugal force.

The first airline to order the Rolls-Royce engine was Cathay Pacific — which specified RB211-524Gs for the first two airframes, and the more-powerful RB211-524H for the third and all subsequent aircraft: finally, in order to standardise the fleet, the first two were returned to the workshops for upgrading. British Airways, Qantas and Air New Zealand had existing fleets of Rolls-Royce powered 747-200s or -300s, and all three continued their alliance with Derby by ordering RB211-524Gs for their new 747-400s. South African Airways later became a new Rolls-Royce customer when it chose the RB211-524H.

Since the 747-400 went into service, all three engine manufacturers have suffered problems of one sort or another, and each has been forced to take corrective action to restore either specific fuel consumption or maintenance-standards guarantees. During the mid-1990s, Pratt & Whitney began

ABOVE: CF6 engines on Asiana 747-48E Combi HL7423. *Gerry Manning*

ABOVE RIGHT: Qantas went for Rolls-Royce RB211-524 engines. *Leo Marriott*

RIGHT: PW 4000 series engines seen on Singapore Airlines 747-412 9V-SPI taking-off from Heathrow. *Rob Holder*

work on what the company later called the 'No.1 Reliability Program', which was designed to improve the in-flight shut-down and unplanned removal rate of all versions of the PW4000-series. Most of the problems were caused by cracking of high-pressure compressor and turbine components; fan-blade fracturing; failures of the auxiliary gearbox bearing, and unexplained surges. The rolling programme of engine upgrades, which used some of the technology developed for the larger PW4084 and PW4168 (Boeing 777/Airbus A330) pow-erplants, has had a dramatic effect on shutdown and gone a long way towards restoring the overall reliability of the engine.

General Electric fitted new, low-emission combustors to the CF6-80C2 during 1996, and a substantial batch of these was later found to be defective and prone to fatigue cracking in one small component. More than 200 engines were finally involved, and repairs had to be undertaken before 1,000 cycles (start-up to shut-down) had been completed. Repair centres were set up in USA, Germany and Singapore, and at the time of writing most of the faulty components had been replaced.

Problems with the Rolls-Royce RB211-524G/H engines began in the early 1990s with several in-flight failures of the original '2B-standard' high-pressure turbine blades — causing engine removal for overhaul after only 1,400 cycles, instead of the anticipated industry-average of 2,000-plus. The original fix for this problem was a new '2C' single-crystal HP blade, which was first offered to the airlines in 1994. Unfortunately, this too, suffered a small number of (shroud) failures. In addition to turbine-blade problems, the engines seemed to be affected by premature ageing, which resulted in

higher than expected fuel consumption and lower exhaust-gas temperatures: this gradual degradation of performance led to reduced power being available for hot-and-high take-offs, which resulted in occasional payload restrictions.

After looking at a number of piecemeal solutions, Derby decided to offer the airlines a significant upgrade of all existing RB211-524H or G engines, based on the core (04-mod-ule) of the newer technology Trent 700 (one of the three option-al powerplants for the Airbus A330). Rolls-Royce say that the new core will reduce RB211 fuel consumption by a further 2 percent, and resolve all of the past reliability problems: as a bonus, the resulting RB211-524G-T or RB211-524H-T instal-lation would save about 880lb (400kg) per aircraft. At the time of writing, SAA and Cathay Pacific have both selected the upgraded engine for new-production 747-400s, and have decid-ed to retrofit all their existing engines as they come up for over-haul: British Airways has agreed to the new-aircraft option, but is 'negotiating' about the cost of a fleet-wide retrofit programme.

NEW NACELLES AND PYLONS

The three powerplant options on the 747-400 are also available on the twin-engined 767, and this has allowed Boeing to provide

a degree of cross-programme commonality. The engine pylons and nacelles on the 747-400 have been re-designed to incorporate the same attachments and services pick-up points (for systems such as fuel, electrics, pneumatics, etc) as those on the 767. This has helped the airlines to reduce their spares holdings, and allows complete powerplant/nacelle combinations to be fully interchangeable between the two types of aircraft. This interchangeability has proved to be particularly valuable to some carriers that use their 767s on extended-range twin-engine operations (ETOPS/EROPS): in this situation, a factory-fresh or recently overhauled engine might be used during the early part of its life on the twin, and later in the overhaul cycle be transferred to the four-engined 747 — where the remote possibility of failure will have less serious consequences. As part of the overall drag-reduction effort, the pylons and nacelles of the 747-400 have also undergone detail aerodynamic improvements.

SURGE TANK AND VENT

FRONT SPAR

REAR SPAR

FUEL TANK*
3300 U.S. GALLONS (12 490 liters)
UP TO 350 NMI RANGE INCREASE

* TAIL FUEL IS REQUIRED FOR TAKEOFF WEIGHTS OF 870,000 LB (394 625 kg)

ABOVE: The horizontal tail fuel tank is an unusual element of the 747-400. Fuel from this tank is pumped into the centre section tank before being distributed to the engines. *Boeing*

RIGHT: The huge 747 tail stands as tall as a four-storey building, providing a massive canvas for airlines to display their colours. Illuminated at night by lamps at the end of the tailplanes, bright tail logos are an ideal recognition feature in crowded airspace. As the registration number identifies, this tail belongs to British Airways 747-436 G-CIVK. *Robbie Shaw*

FUEL SYSTEM

The fuel system hardware in the 747-400 — at least in the wing and centre-fuselage — is not too far removed from the equivalent system on earlier models, but most of the tanks, sensors, valves and fuel-lines have been changed in small ways to accommodate the automatic 'set-and-forget' functions of digital fuel management. All contents, flows and temperatures are now continually monitored by the system, and the transfer of fuel to alleviate wing bending stresses is now a fully automatic process: if manual intervention is required, pilots can access the system at any time via the overhead panel. The 747-400 now has an optional 2,747gal (12,490 litres) tank in the horizontal stabilizer: this feeds directly into the centre-wing tank, and gives the aircraft an additional 340nm (650km) range at normal cruise altitude. The stabilizer tank is not used for trimming the aircraft in flight (as on Airbus), but it must be full to achieve take-off at optional gross weights in excess of 850,000lb (385,000kg). At the end of each sector, the flight management computer automatically sets the variable incidence tailplane to the optimum position for refuelling. The total usable fuel capacity of the 747-400 is 47,605gal (216,389 litres).

THE TAIL

In addition to the new fuel tank, several other changes were incorporated around the tail of the 747-400. The overall geometry of the tail remained the same, but because of the extra weight of the aircraft, the maximum rudder-deflection angle was increased from 25° to 30° each side: this reduced the minimum control speed on the ground (V^{mcg}) by about 10kts, which was universally welcomed by pilots. The control configuration of the split-section rudder was also amended: instead of both sections having a dual/tandem actuator system, the new aircraft was designed with three actuators and a triple control-valve on the upper rudder, and two actuators and a dual-valve on the lower. The balance weights on the upper rudder were considered unnecessary, and removed altogether.

THE NEW APU

Much to the surprise of everyone who knew the aircraft, Boeing selected Pratt & Whitney of Canada to supply a new and untried auxiliary power unit (APU) for the 747-400, rather than staying with the Garrett (now Allied Signal Aerospace) units that had been fitted to every 747 since production began: furthermore, the new PW901A was chosen straight off the drawing board, and it was P&WC's first venture into the APU market for some years. It was based on the core of the popular JT15D turbofan, but incorporated a new power-turbine to drive the load compressor and gearbox. Installed in the tailcone of a 747, the APU supplies all the electrical and pneumatic needs of the aircraft, when the main engines are shut down. On the 747-400, the PW901A drives two Bendix 28/263 air-cooled 90kVA generators, which between them provide enough power to eliminate all load-shedding problems from the aircraft — a valuable asset on a two-man flightdeck. The air system delivers enough pneumatic power to start two of the main propulsion engines at the same time; and enough conditioned air to maintain the passenger cabin temperature at 75°F, while the aircraft is parked in full sun on a 100°F day. On a big aircraft like the 747-400 these small engines are required to work hard, and the APU may actually be running for upwards of 2,500hr per year.

The manufacturers claim that the PW901A does this with appreciably less noise and pollution than earlier APUs, and with a 40 percent reduction in fuel consumption.

ELECTRICAL SYSTEM

The main electrical supply on the 747-400 is essentially unchanged from the well-proven system used on first-generation aircraft, but the management of the system can now be fully automatic if required. All four flight engines drive 90kVa Sundstrand generators, which are fitted with 757/767-style integrated drives: these provide the AC supply to four output busses, which are isolated and switched automatically to enable each bus to remain powered, even when its individual generator is not operating. All trimming and load-shedding functions are fully automated, and faults in any part of the system are now detected, identified and isolated before any crew action becomes necessary: appropriate EICAS alerts will appear, and CMC failure-modes will be stored for later analysis by maintenance personnel. AC systems switches on the overhead panel will allow the flight crew to override a certain number of the automatic functions if necessary. Each main AC bus powers a transformer/rectifier unit which provides power to one of four DC busses, each of which operate on the same interconnection principles as the AC system. In the event of main-engine or generator failure, system overloads are prevented by automatic load-shedding to a programmed sequence, which continues until the possible overload condition is relieved: while this sequence is in operation the upper EICAS screen keeps the crew informed. In the event of a major failure, or combination of failures, a full synoptics display of the electrical system is available.

UNDERCARRIAGE

The unique landing-gear configuration of the 747 has been carried forward from all the earlier models, but the increased take-off weight of the new 400-series — and the digital nature of most of its systems — has led to a number of important detail changes. The most significant of these was the adoption of carbon brake units, which had already been proved by Boeing on the twin-jet 757. These are a great deal more costly than multi-disc steel brakes, but they save 1,800lb (818kg) weight per ship-set, and last about twice as long before service renewal becomes necessary. More importantly perhaps — in view of the higher operating weights of a 747-400 — the available brake energy has been increased by about 15 percent. The overall diameter

ABOVE RIGHT: Virgin Atlantic's G-VTOP *Virginia Plain* taking-off. Note the APU exhaust in the tail; the 747-400's APU is the PW901A; all previous 747 types used Garrett (Allied Signal Aerospace) units. Note the deployment of the leading edge slats, which increase the wing area on take-off thus increasing lift. On the fuselage near the tail the 'No way BA/AA' refers to the intended code-sharing arrangement between the two companies which Virgin boss Richard Branson views with great displeasure. *Geoff Harber*

RIGHT: EVA Air B-16401 takes-off from Miami, Florida. Note undercarriage doors open and wheels beginning to retract. *Geoff Harber*

ABOVE: Air Canada C-GAGL lands at Heathrow. The 747-400 undercarriage has to withstand a significant weight increase as compared to earlier models. *Geoff Harber*

LEFT: This British Airways 747-436 on lift off from Everett is half way through its gear retraction sequence, with the undercarriage doors just starting to open preparatory to wheel retraction. *Boeing*

ABOVE RIGHT: The 747-400 wheel discs have to be 2in (5cm) bigger than those of the Classic to accommodate the larger carbon brakes. *Boeing*

RIGHT: The two-man cockpit of the 747-400. *Robbie Shaw*

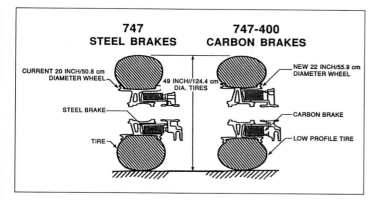

747
STEEL BRAKES

747-400
CARBON BRAKES

CURRENT 20 INCH/50.8 cm
DIAMETER WHEEL

NEW 22 INCH/55.9 cm
DIAMETER WHEEL

49 INCH/124.4 cm
DIA. TIRES

STEEL BRAKE

CARBON BRAKE

TIRE

LOW PROFILE TIRE

of the main wheel/tyre combination on the 747 has always been limited to 49in (1.25m) by existing clearances in the wheel bay. It was not possible to change this on the 747-400, but the new brakes had to be physically bigger than the old steel units, and still fit in the same space. To accommodate them, Boeing increased the diameter of the metal wheel-disc from 20in to 22in (0.51 to 0.57m), and adopted a new low-profile tyre.

As a result of the digitisation of the 747-400's major systems, the undercarriage and brakes are now far more sophisticated in operation. The old manual lock for the body gear steering has been replaced by an automatic system, which keeps the inner gear locked in the straight-ahead position until the taxi speed has dropped to below 15kts: at this point the trucks are automatically unlocked, and will start to turn in the opposite direction to the nosewheel when the tiller deflection angle exceeds 20°. On take-off, the locks are automatically re-engaged as soon as the aircraft accelerates through 20kt. Nosewheel steering through the rudder pedals is limited to 7°. The brakes

are now fitted with a digital anti-skid system which is more sensitive and much cleaner in operation: this has less tendency to grab, and therefore helps to reduce tyre wear. A brand new amenity on the -400 series aircraft is the French (Labinal) tyre pressure indicating system (TPIS), which constantly monitors the pressure of each individual tyre and displays an immediate alert if any one of them looks like reaching an upper or lower pre-set limit. This system is optional, but most operators are having it installed because a single tyre-burst incident can cause a huge amount of costly airframe damage. Most pilots agree that the 747 is now much easier to handle on the ground: the carbon brakes are considerably less jerky in operation, the tyres are better protected, and the new winglets make the wingtips much more visible.

TWO-CREW COCKPIT

The 747-400 flightdeck represents the most radical change to the whole aircraft — with virtually nothing left of the original layout, save the position of the two pilot's seats. The flight engineer's desk, with its large instrument and control panel, has now completely gone from the starboard side, and the whole cockpit area looks considerably less cluttered. All the engineer's 'house-keeping' functions have now been fully automated, and transferred to a single overhead panel.

Boeing is a strangely conservative organisation, and the engineers at Seattle took some persuading before they agreed to convert the 747 to digital avionics — despite their pioneering efforts with the 757 and 767 cockpits. Both of these twin-jet aircraft had been given virtually the same electronic systems, and

ANALOG 747s

DIGITAL 747-400s

MAIN PICTURE: The new flightdeck is a vast improvement over the older three-crew version. Here the captain has his hands on the throttle quadrants. *Boeing*

INSET LEFT: Comparison drawing between the analog (electro-mechanical) instrumentation of the old flightdeck and the cleaner, more modern EFIS cockpit. *Boeing*

INSET RIGHT: Cockpit of an old 747 showing the size of the flight engineer's station; all the instrumentation has now been condensed, automated and moved to the pilots' overhead panel. (Captain's seat has been removed for clarity.) *Boeing*

both were selling well to home and export markets — often together, enabling the airlines to take advantage of a common crew-training environment. The obvious first thoughts on conversion of the 747 were focused on a continuation of the already-proven 757/767 system: this used an electronic attitude director indicator (EADI) to display attitude information derived from the inertial reference system, and an electronic horizontal situation indicator (EHSI) to display navigational information. Together, these formed the electronic flight instrumentation system (EFIS), which was presented to the pilots on two separate screens, placed vertically above each other. In addition to the EFIS, the 757/767 cockpit had a twin-screen engine indication and crew alerting system (EICAS) mounted centrally between the pilots: this displayed all the engines and systems information, and gathered together all the usual caution and warning signals. Most of this system was later used to update the 737-300, and there must have been a great deal of pressure to use it again on the digital version of the 747.

Airbus Industries, meanwhile, had begun to incorporate air data (altitude and airspeed) on the CRT screens of its new A320, and this move was greatly welcomed by most airline accountants because it reduced even more the number of expensive mechanical instruments on the flightdeck. After a round of discussions with some of its 747 customers, Boeing turned away from the tempting possibility of providing a common flightdeck on all four of its major airliners, and opted for larger screens showing as much information as possible. The earlier EADI subsequently became the 747-400's primary flight display (PFD), and the EHSI was transformed into the navigation display (ND). At 8in (20cm) square the 747-400 screens are about half as big again as those used in the EFIS cockpits of the 757, 767 and updated 737-300: because of this, the PFD and ND were positioned side-by-side in front of each pilot,

RIGHT: Layout of pilots' instruments showing overhead panel, main panel and aisle stand and the distribution of the main flight management controls. *Boeing*

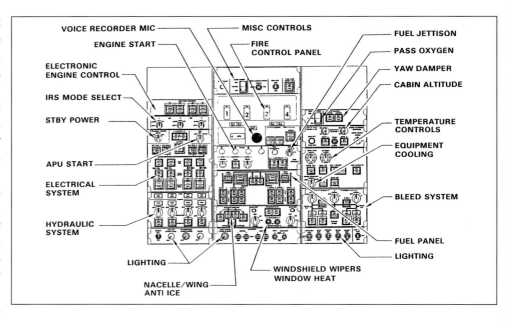

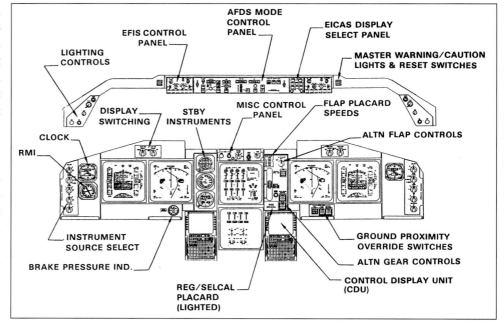

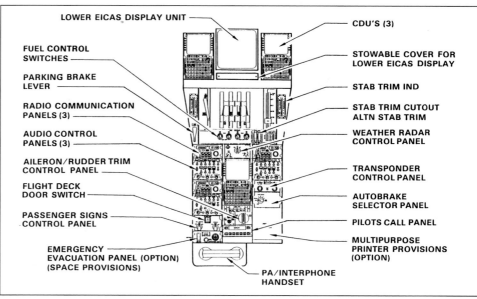

instead of one above the other. The EICAS screens were still positioned vertically in the centre of the main panel, but the larger format made the presentation of data from four engines clearer.

PRIMARY FLIGHT DISPLAY

The 747-400's primary flight display (PFD) consists of a cathode ray tube presentation of all the 'basic-T' flight instruments (attitude, altitude, airspeed and vertical speed), plus a heading (compass) display, and a number of functions that were previously dealt with by separate instruments or indicator lights. The display is dominated by the 3.25in (8.3cm) wide x 3.5in (8.9cm) high attitude indicator (artificial horizon), which shows aircraft attitude information derived from the inertial reference system (IRS). This is now presented in a rectangular format because NASA research suggested that this gave pilots an improved awareness of their situation, especially during a climbing or descending turn. The attitude display is flanked by a vertical 'tape' airspeed indicator on the left, and a similar altimeter and separate vertical speed indicator on the right. The airspeed tape has normal 10kt graduations, but a central expanded-digit box displays current speed to an accuracy of 1kt: a useful speed-trend arrow extends up or down from this box, to show the predicted speed in 10sec at the current rate of acceleration or deceleration. Take-off speed 'bugs' are generated by the flight management computer (FMC) when the zero-fuel and block-fuel weights are entered into the system, and these appear on the tape in their correct linear position. The approach of 'red-line' speeds (stick-shaker operation, gear or flap limits, Vmo, etc) are signalled to the pilots by a simple change of colour, which makes many of the audible warnings unnecessary. All airspeed information on the PFD is derived from the air data computer (ADC).

The vertical tape altimeter is the same size on the PFD as the airspeed indicator. It displays barometric altitude derived from the air data computers, with its normal readout showing tape divisions every 100ft (30.5m): the expanded-digit current altitude box changes scale to give 20ft (6.1m) divisions. When the aircraft descends below 2,500ft/762.5m (above ground level) a digital display of radio-altitude automatically appears alongside the normal pressure-altitude tape: an approach decision-height reminder can also be displayed if required. The all-important *selected altitude* (the altitude to which a pilot is currently cleared by ATC) appears in digital form above the rolling tape display, and the tape itself is flagged to provide advance warning of its approach. The current barometric setting of the altimeter system is displayed in a box below the graduated scale. To assist the transition between western and the old eastern-bloc ATC environments, the whole altitude display can be converted to metric at the touch of a button.

On the extreme right of the PFD, the vertical-speed display uses a logarithmic scale that expands as it gets closer to the zero (level-flight) position, making it much easier to read when the pilots are monitoring a non-precision approach. The display derives its data from the IRS, and has an overall scale that covers 6,000ft (1,830m)/min up or down. An accurate four-digit

numerical readout is shown whenever the vertical speed exceeds 400ft (122m)/min: these numbers appear directly above the main display while the aircraft is climbing, and below it during the descent.

The aircraft-heading information is displayed at the bottom of the PFD, directly beneath the attitude indicator. Before presenting this in the traditional compass-rose style display — rather than a flat tape — Boeing talked to a large number of airline pilots to find out which they preferred. The selected (autopilot-derived) heading is shown as a 'bug' on the periphery of the rotating arc, and as a digital readout alongside the heading-reference data (magnetic or true). To make them more immediately visible, the current-heading digits wind through an expanded-scale box — in exactly the same way as those of the airspeed and altitude displays.

Since it first appeared on the 747-400, the primary flight display has been upgraded to incorporate several new warning systems. Most aircraft now have TCAS (traffic-alert and collision avoidance system) pitch commands overlaid in red on the attitude indicator display, and TCAS vertical speed cues (again in red) on the vertical speed display. These are automatically triggered by a potential air traffic conflict, and tell the pilots where it is safe to fly in order to avoid a collision: the pilots of the 'intruder' aircraft (if it is TCAS-equipped) will receive similar guidance, and because the two systems 'talk' to each other, they will mutually ensure a vertically diverging flight path. All potential conflict situations are accompanied by one of 12 voice annunciations, ranging from an initial 'Traffic, Traffic', to the rather more urgent 'Climb — climb now. Climb — climb now'. A plan view of surrounding TCAS-equipped traffic can also be called up on certain modes of the navigation display.

Three modes of the conventional ground proximity warning system (GPWS) also issue red alert warnings on the

BELOW: Primary flight display. *Boeing*

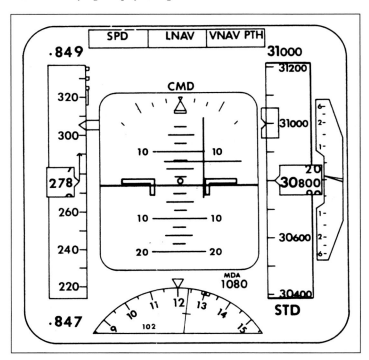

primary flight display (in the screen area between the base of the attitude display and the top of the compass arc). These are always accompanied by aural alerts, and by associated instrument panel warning lights. If the barometric sink rate becomes too severe, or if the aircraft is threatened with flying into high ground, the GPWS voice annunciation 'Whoop. Whoop. Pull Up' sounds; the master caution/warning lights illuminate, and the message PULL UP is displayed on both PFDs. When any significant down-draft or rapidly changing wind condition is detected during take-off or landing the voice reports 'Windshear' three times; the master caution/warning lights snap on, and a red WINDSHEAR message appears on both screens. Recently an upgraded version of GPWS — the enhanced ground proximity warning system, or EGPWS has been introduced by a number of airlines. This compares the geographical position of the aircraft (derived from the flight management system), and its known altitude (from the air data system), with terrain elevations stored in the EGPWS computer data-base: this system is constantly monitored by the aircraft's radio altimeter, and can provide a full-colour display of terrain close to the flight path (although not on the primary flight display).

NAVIGATION DISPLAY

The navigation display on the 747-400 has four standard operating modes — approach, VOR, map and plan — plus secondary modes showing a full compass rose overlaid on the approach, VOR and map displays. The system still retains many of the features designed for the 757 and 767, but it now has double the maximum range (out to 640 miles (1,030km) — which has proved to be a great advantage on today's longer-range 'direct' routings), and a new look-behind capability to

BELOW: Captain's instrument panel navigation display shown in map mode. *Boeing*

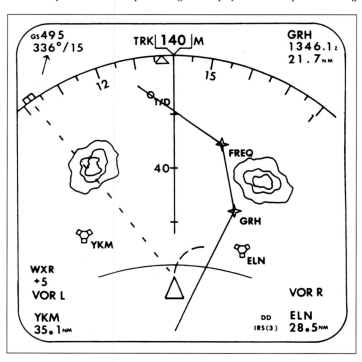

ease the problems of manoeuvring in restricted airspace. The multi-colour weather-radar picture can be superimposed on the approach, VOR and map displays.

The two ND screens are normally located inboard of the primary flight displays. Heading and track information is drawn from the duplicated inertial reference system and flight management computers respectively, with the captain's screen feeding from the left-hand IRS/FMC, and the co-pilot's from the right. The map mode is normally selected for day-to-day route flying. This has a 90° expanded compass arc at the top, and the rest of the display has all the benefits of a continuously moving aeronautical chart, which gives the aircraft's current position and heading against a background of fixed flight-plan way points; relevant navigational aids (selected and tuned by the FMC); external influences on the flight such as wind direction and strength, and returns from the weather-radar. The positions and frequencies of all suitable ground-based navaids along the route (VOR, DME/TACAN and VORTAC) are held in the data-base of the FMC, and these are tuned automatically by the system as required: the signals are then used to update the IRS/FMC. To guard against the possibility of complete FMC failure, the pilots can still manually tune navaids. If the aircraft develops any kind of major *en route* problem, every airport in the area with a runway of 5,000ft (1,525m) or more can be called up on the ND as a possible diversionary field.

The conventional VOR and approach modes of the navigation display (VOR for *en route* navigation, and approach for ILS landings) have the 90° compass arc at the top, and both displays are shown heading up, instead of the more modern track Up format of the map presentation. Both modes are essentially available to cover the unlikely event of an FMC failure, or perhaps the lack of a particular data-base (an aircraft owned by a leasing company, for example, may not be equipped with an expensive data-base for China, but occasional contracts could take it into that part of the world). Without the data-base facility, manual tuning of all ground-based aids is essential, but both modes can still accept the overlaid weather picture — unless the pilots have selected the full compass rose presentation, in which case the weather display is inhibited.

The plan mode displays a static, true-north up, depiction of the entire departure-to-touchdown route, which is accessed through the 'legs' pages of the FMC. The upper part of the display is the same as that in map mode (showing the 90° track up compass arc with its current heading and reference), but the lower portion shows the planned route — generally on multiple pages. The primary operational use of this mode is the mandatory pre-departure checking of the route (as input by the flight crew or drawn from the data-base): any mistakes should be spotted and rectified at this stage, or the aircraft could find itself heading for the wrong destination. The weather-radar information has no relevance to this display, and is therefore inhibited.

FLIGHT MANAGEMENT SYSTEM

The flight management system (FMS) on the 747-400 integrates most of the sub-systems which help the pilots to control (or manage) the lateral and vertical flight path of the aircraft — normally referred to as Lnav and Vnav. The FMS provides automatic navigation functions; in-flight performance monitoring and 'fine-tuning'; automatic monitoring of the fuel system, and organises the accurate presentation of information on the cockpit displays. Central to the whole system is the duplicated Honeywell/Sperry flight management computer (FMC). This uses details input by the pilots (the flight plan); active data from a range of supporting sub-systems; and information stored on the data-base, to calculate the present position of the aircraft: it then interprets commands issued by the pilots, and sends appropriate pitch, roll and thrust commands to enable the aircraft to follow an accurate flight profile. The supporting sub-systems and data sources include the inertial reference system; the air data computer; the electronic engine control (Fadec) systems; fuel flows and quantities; electronic clock and input from various navigation beacons. Outgoing commands from the FMC are addressed to the autopilot, autothrottle and flight director, and its information is used to continuously update the primary-flight and navigation displays.

An extensive database is essential to the operation of these electronic flight instrumentation systems. The information stored in the 747-400 FMC is divided into two major sections one dealing with navigation, and the other specifically with performance-related data. The navigation section includes most of the information that the pilots would normally expect to get from aeronautical charts, plus a number of airline-selected (optional) items. Basically the airline gets what it pays for, but a comprehensive data-base can include the location, frequencies and identifiers of VHF navaids; details of all 747 compatible airports (and even their individual runways, together with information about the operational status of various landing aids); instructions on standard instrument departure and arrival routes (SIDs and STARs), and full details of so-called company routes: these are flown so often by an airline that they can generally be programmed into the system as complete departure to arrival flight-plans, which avoids the need to key-in each separate waypoint. The coverage of the system is potentially worldwide, but each patch has to be updated every 28 days to ensure its compliance with conventional aeronautical charts. This revision process makes data-base maintenance a costly business, and most airlines will select only those patches that directly relate to their normal route network.

Access to the computer is through one of the alpha-numeric keyboards of the FMS control and display units (FMS-CDUs) sometimes called the multi-function control and display unit (MCDU). Each pilot is supplied with one of these devices, mounted at knee-level on the forward aisle-stand and flanking the lower EICAS screen. At the start of each flight, the FMS-CDU — which has a display screen at the top and a keyboard below is used to enter the complete flight-plan, together with load sheet details, and any routes, waypoints, departure or arrival patterns that are not already held on the data-base. Airborne flight-plan amendments are also entered via the FMS-CDUs, and several specialised pages of prompts are available to speed the two-way flow of information needed for

ATC requests to go direct, change climb conditions, enter or exit holding patterns, etc. The system can also be used to calculate the advantages (or otherwise) of new routes or altitudes if they are offered by ATC: the computer will do all the donkey work, and display its predictions before the pilots

COMMUNICATIONS

Most 747-400s are equipped with three VHF and two HF communications radios, all of which can be selected and tuned by any one of three individual radio control panels: separate multi-function audio control panels (ACPs) are used to actually transmit and receive on any of the radios. The ACPs also allow the pilots to talk to ground crew during turn-round operations; to use the cabin interphone or passenger address system, and to monitor selected navigation receivers.

In addition to voice communications, an increasing number of aircraft are fitted with the Airborne Communication Addressing and Reporting System (ACARS) — which allows operational text messages to be received and transmitted almost anywhere in the world. The ACARS system operates as an integral part of the overall flight management system (FMS), and its primary function is to provide a constant channel of communication between the aircraft and its own airline operations centre. The system normally uses VHF frequencies to 'talk' to one of several world-wide ground stations, where an ACARS service provider will relay the message to the appropriate Ops Centre and wait for a reply (if needed): the reply is then re-transmitted to the aircraft. Messages can also go in the opposite direction (Ops Centre to aircraft).

Systems that support ACARS include the central maintenance computer (CMC); the aircraft condition monitoring system (ACMS), and the flight management computer (FMC): together these three units hold a comprehensive picture of what the aircraft is doing at any one time — and how well it is doing it. Selected data (related, for example, to engine health monitoring) can be drawn from the supporting systems and automatically transmitted to the engineering staff at the airline's operations centre: in this way, an engineer sitting at a desk in London might be able to tell an aircraft-commander somewhere over the Pacific, that his No.2 engine is showing the first signs of a rear-bearing failure.

ACARS is also linked to an accurate clock, and will automatically transmit such information as the times of gate departure, take-off, landing and gate-arrival. In addition to automatic messages, the flight crew (or Ops Centre) can initiate either 'required' messages (standard-format presentations of load sheets, flight plans, etc), or 'freetext' messages — which can cover almost everything, from requests for weather information, to news of a passenger becoming unwell. When an incoming message reaches the aircraft a chime sounds on the flight-deck; a call-light appears on the audio control panel, and an alert message appears on the upper EICAS screen. Because ACARS is basically a text system, most messages are received via a dedicated printer on the central aisle stand. ACARS is still a relatively new piece of equipment, and people are still discovering new ways of using it.

CENTRAL MAINTENANCE COMPUTER

Over the years, 100, 200 and 300-series 747s had been fitted with a variety of different built-in test equipment (BITE) systems — the majority of which found a home on the flight engineer's panel. Now that the 747-400 is a two-crew aeroplane, the engineer's monitoring functions have been absorbed into several automatic systems, and the duplicated central maintenance computer (CMC) is a vital part of this reorganisation. A third 'spare' FMS-CDU is located on the central aisle stand, between the pilot's seats: this unit is identical in every respect to the two used to communicate with the flight management system (and indeed, can be used as a reserve in the event of a failure in one of the primaries) but its main task is to act as an interface with the CMC.

Using a sophisticated digital-databus in place of miles of heavy wiring, the CMC now links all the important aircraft systems, and acts as a central clearing-house for many different kinds of performance-monitoring signals. The incoming information can be analysed and translated into a plain-language readout (*ILS No. 1 Antenna Inop*, for example), and displayed on the screen of the CDU. If a significant problem arises, the pilots can use the CDU keyboard to select various synoptics diagrams for display on the lower EICAS screen. These pages show schematic representations of the current status of all major aircraft systems (electrics, fuel, hydraulics, landing-gear, etc), and are designed to help the crew trace the source of the problem, and then take whatever remedial action is possible. Information held on the CMC is later made available to the maintenance engineers, which has greatly eased their task of fault rectification. In case it proves too much of a distraction during a difficult approach, the CMC cannot be accessed by the crew while the aircraft is below 10,000ft (3,050m).

EICAS

The basic configuration of the engine indication and crew alerting system (EICAS) on the 747-400 was developed from the system first used on the 757 and 767. The 747 is obviously a bigger and far more complex aeroplane than either of the twinjets, so the display-screens are larger and all the software has been completely renewed. The basic task of the system is to permanently replace all four sets of mechanical engine instruments, although its operational usefulness has gone far beyond that. As soon as electrical power is applied to the system (during the pre-flight preparations) the upper EICAS screen shows the primary engine indications (EPR/N1 and EGT = engine pressure ratio, fan-shaft speed, and exhaust gas temperature), and the lower screen shows the secondary engine indications (N2 or N2/N3 shaft speeds; fuel flows; oil pressures, temperatures and quantities, and engine vibration levels). The primary indications remain on the screen throughout the flight, but the secondaries can be replaced at any time by other EICAS displays from the FMC/CMC repertoire. The computers continuously monitor the secondary indicators whenever the engines are running, and if an 'amber-line' reading is sensed, the crew is alerted by a short beeper noise to attract attention; an appropriate caution message on the upper screen; and an abbreviated version of the secondary engine display which is automatically returned to the lower screen whenever a potential problem is detected. Most airlines have chosen the vertical tape format for these displays, but the round dial-type is still available as a customer option. In both cases the graphical presentation provides a quick glance relative value only: accurate *numerical* values are shown alongside each tape presentation.

Crew-selectable primary aircraft status information (such as door positions; tyre pressures and brake temperatures; landing-gear and flap positions, etc) can be displayed on the upper screen, alongside the primary engine data. Also on this screen are the warning, caution and advisory messages of the crew alerting system. EICAS has more than 100 alert conditions on its menu, virtually all of which are inhibited to some degree during part of the take-off sequence (messages will still appear on the screen, but the attention-grabbing lights and noises are suppressed to avoid crew distraction). All alarms for cautionary messages are suppressed as soon as the aircraft reaches 80kt on the runway, and they remain quiet until 800ft (244m) or 30sec after take-off — whichever occurs first.

Conditions that would normally generate a full warning message are obviously more critical: the suppression of full alarms in this case is delayed until the aircraft has reached V1, and everything is reactivated at 400ft (122m) or take-off/+25sec. If a fire-warning message occurs during this high-workload phase of take-off, the normal warning lights and bell are activated as soon as the inhibit period ends.

All EICAS alert conditions are generated by automatic monitoring of the aircraft systems, and each is given a pre-arranged priority which depends on its requirement for corrective action. Warning messages relate to any condition that immediately threatens the integrity of the aircraft or the safety of its occupants: these include such things as cabin decompression; fire; excess aircraft speed; uncommanded autopilot disconnection, etc. Warning messages are all accompanied by the illumination of master caution/warning lights on the pilots' glareshield, and by one or other of the audible alarms (a bell for fire; siren for overspeed and wailer for autopilot disconnect, etc). The message itself will appear at the top of the EICAS screen in red. Pressing either of the caution/warning switchlights will re-arm the system for any further alerts, but the warning message itself will not vanish from the EICAS screen until the condition that triggered it has been resolved.

Cautionary messages draw attention to any condition that needs timely action by the pilots, but does not threaten immediate escalation or danger. These appear on the screen in amber — below the last of the red warning messages — and are always signalled by a short beeper sound and the illumination of both master caution/warning lights. There are nearly 50 cautions in the system, alerting the pilots to such items as generator failure; low hydraulic pressure; nacelle icing; smoke in one of the lavatories, etc.

Advisory messages have the lowest priority of all, and do not trigger audible alarms or the master caution/warning lights. These mostly represent temporary or minor conditions, and often serve as simple reminders that, for instance, passenger

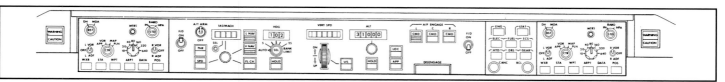

ABOVE: Detail of autopilot mode control panel showing the EFIS control panels and beyond them the master caution/warning lights. This sits on the centre of the glare shield allowing both pilots to operate the autopilot. (See page 54 middle drawing for cockpit location.) *Boeing*

doors are still open or the parking brake is still on. Other advisories inform the pilots that computer monitoring has detected a fault in one of the primary aircraft systems, and automatically switched over to a reserve system: any such failures will also be recorded on the CMC, for later action by the maintenance staff. Advisory alerts appear on the screen in amber, but insert one character-space to detach them from cautions.

All EICAS alert messages have a very clear and logical order of priority. Warnings (red) are always listed at the top of the screen; cautions (amber) appear below the last of the warnings, and advisories (amber/offset) are listed below the last of the cautions. When a new message is received it automatically appears at the top of its category, pushing everything below it down one line. When a condition no longer exists — autopilot reconnected, for example — its message disappears, and everything below it moves up one line. Multiple message-pages can be sequenced through the screen by using the keyboard of the FMS-CDU.

DISPLAY SCREENS

The six cathode-ray display screens for the EFIS/EICAS on the 747-400 are identical, and fully interchangeable within the aircraft. To save weight and space each screen has its own integrated signal generator, and pin-select connectors determine its ultimate function within the instrument panel layout. The overall screen brightness level can be set by the pilots at any time, and an automatic brightness control system will adjust any individual screen (or screens, including the FMS-CDUs) to prevent its display being overwhelmed by bright sunlight. Screen failures obviously occur from time-to-time, and much work was done in the system-planning phase to ensure that these failures would have a minimal effect on the progress of a flight.

Any two screens can fail *en route* without any loss of information to the pilots. Should either of the primary flight displays fail, all of its normal flight instrument data will automatically be transferred to the adjacent navigation display; in a similar way, a primary EICAS failure would result in all the data being switched to the secondary (lower) position. In addition to these automatic functions, both pilots have the ability to manually switch the screen positions around (the navigation display, for instance, could be switched to the lower EICAS position): in this way almost any single failure — or combination of failures — can be accommodated. The aircraft can still be dispatched if only five of the screens are working, but the failed unit must be positioned in the lower EICAS slot before departure. In the unlikely event of all screens failing at the same time, the aircraft has a full set of standby instruments comprising altitude indicator (with approach display); airspeed indicator; altimeter; compass and a radio magnetic indicator (RMI) for VOR and ADF bearings. On the original 747-400s these standby instruments were all electro-mechanical devices, but the latest production aircraft have EFIS-style standby displays, all supplied from a dedicated power source.

AUTOPILOT

The Collins autopilot flight director system (AFDS) on the 747-400 is very similar to that fitted on both the 757 and 767. It comprises three separate (triplex) flight control computers (FCCs), and a single mode control panel (MCP) as the common interface unit for both pilots: the MCP accepts commands for the autopilot; flight director; altitude alert and autothrottle functions of the system. The FCCs issue commands to control servos, which operate the individual flying controls through three separate hydraulic systems. In normal cruising flight the autopilot controls only the ailerons and elevators, but rudder commands and nosewheel steering control are added during the approach to, and roll out from, an automatic landing; and during all go-around manoeuvres. During an ILS approach, all three FCCs are powered from separate electrical sources. Automatic landings (at suitably equipped airports) can be made down to Category 3b standard — which requires no decision height, but must have a runway visual range of at least 246ft (75m) in order to taxi the aircraft to the terminal area.

COCKPIT ENVIRONMENT

From a pilot's point of view, the cockpit environment of a 747-400 is a tremendous advance on all earlier models of the aircraft: everything seems a lot tidier now, and perhaps a little less hurried. In operational terms the older three-crew aircraft had an average of 950 lights, instruments and switches around the flight-deck: these have been condensed into about 365 (depending on equipment standards) in the digital aircraft. It seems certain that an ex-757/767 pilot will feel far more at home in the 747-400 cockpit, than a pilot coming straight from the 'clockwork' environment of the traditional 747.

The pilot's seats have been redesigned, and now give easier access to the main panel: they also have slightly longer fore and-aft tracks than all previous models, giving an extra 3in (7.5cm) of leg-room for long periods of cruising flight. Each pilot has a fold-out desk for meals, charts, and completion of that never-ending supply of airline paperwork: and flight bags — which are still needed, even in the highly sophisticated cockpit of a 747-400 — have their own stowage position outboard of the crew seats. Considerable attention has also been paid to

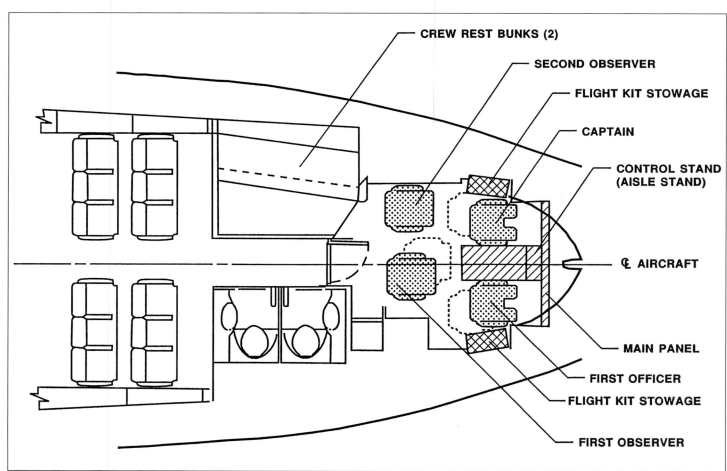

CREW REST BUNKS (2)

SECOND OBSERVER

FLIGHT KIT STOWAGE

CAPTAIN

CONTROL STAND
(AISLE STAND)

℄ AIRCRAFT

MAIN PANEL

FIRST OFFICER

FLIGHT KIT STOWAGE

FIRST OBSERVER

noise reduction around the cockpit. Extra soundproofing has made a marked difference to the external airflow noise, and air-conditioning flows have been improved all round to reduce the familiar 'blast' effect of cockpit-equipment cooling fans.

The 747-400 has significantly more range than most airliners, and the cockpit has undergone several changes to reflect these very long sectors. For obvious safety reasons, all pilots are strictly limited in the number of duty hours they can undertake without adequate periods of rest: the aircraft on the other hand, can easily fly for 15 or 16 hours at a stretch — way beyond the legal endurance of any single crew. This has resulted in the curious anomaly of an aircraft basically designed for two-crew operation, actually carrying three — or perhaps even four — qualified pilots. By sharing the operational flying between them, and getting some rest between periods of duty, an enlarged crew can fly these long sectors without infringing either their own company rules, or the statutory regulations. The flight crew accommodation on the 747-400 now includes two secondary 'observer' seats and an isolated bedroom.

The so-called 'bedroom' is actually a tiny compartment on one side of the main flightdeck area. This room has floor level dimensions of no more than 7ft x 5ft (2.1 x 1.5m), and contains two full-length bunk beds, each with its own passenger-style fresh-air vent and reading lamp. The furnishings are far from luxurious, but the door can at least be closed to provide some degree of isolation from the normal rumble of cockpit noises. Even with complete darkness (there are no windows in this part of the aircraft), some pilots still find it impossible to sleep properly under such artificial conditions, and the best that they can hope for is a period of quiet relaxation.

The question of tiredness among long-range aircrew is now regarded with a much more enlightened attitude than it was some years ago. The official line on this (from the airlines, the regulatory authorities and from the pilots' unions) has always been that the pilots should not fall asleep at the controls. The cockpit of a modern airliner, however, with its fully automatic monitoring of all aircraft systems, and navigation by computer data-base, can be a very soporific environment — especially at night or after a long trip through difficult time zones. Recent studies in aviation medicine have clearly shown the physiological benefits of 'cat-napping' during a long flight, and it has now become more or less acceptable for one pilot to nod off for a few minutes in the cruise, while the other minds the shop: both pilots have to agree to this, and the pilot who remains at the controls must be able to wake his colleague — especially if he too feels drowsy.

When Boeing engineers were preparing equipment and software for the 747-400 flightdeck, they realised that there was a remote danger of both pilots falling asleep at the same time, and incorporated a crew alertness monitor into the flight management system. This keeps a watching brief on several panels and switches that would normally be used during the progress of a flight: if no movement is detected on any of these during a specified time, an EICAS advisory message appears, asking for some kind of *pilot response*. If there is still no crew activity, the message

is upgraded to a caution, and the normal caution audible alert sounds: if this is further ignored, the EICAS goes into full warning mode, with illumination of the master caution/warning lights and an audible alarm. The system only operates during the cruise at 20,000ft (6,100m) or above, and its monitoring function keeps track of any crew activity on the VHF/HF radio control panels; the EFIS/EICAS control panels; the AFDS mode control panel, and the left or right FMS control and display unit. Any response on any of these panels will cancel the EICAS message, and reset the system for another period of monitoring.

The two observer seats in the cockpit are generally used by the extra 'cruise-pilots' during take-off and landing, but are often occupied by training or check captains: both positions can also be used for taking off-duty meals. They are also useful during duty handover periods, when the incoming pilot can overlook the current crew, and familiarise himself with the aircraft situation. One of the seats is in a fixed position on the left-hand side of the cockpit, directly behind, but slightly higher than, the captain's seat; the other is mounted on a short track that allows it to move diagonally forward, until it reaches a position on the aircraft centreline and immediately aft of the aisle-stand.

THE 'ATTIC' BEDROOM

Although the dangers of crew fatigue are more generally associated with pilots, an alert cabin crew is vital to the smooth running of any passenger aircraft — particularly in the unlikely event of something going horribly wrong. The 747-400 will often carry up to 20 cabin attendants on a very long sector, and they too will need adequate rest periods during the course of a 15-hour working day. As a customer option on the 747-400, Boeing engineers designed a dedicated rest area for cabin crew which is now known as the 'attic' bedroom because it occupies part of the main cabin roof-space, directly beneath the base of the fin. This room is much larger than the cockpit equivalent, and can be equipped with two, four or eight bunk beds, together with optional arrangements of standard or sleeper seats. All bunks can be individually curtained off, and the lighting system has been designed to provide anything between near-daylight conditions and almost total darkness: extra sound insulation has also been provided, but the airflow-split around the base of the vertical tail still creates more noise in that area than the designers had hoped. Access to the attic is via a short stairway on the starboard side of the fuselage.

The attic is not a standard fit on all passenger versions of the 747-400, but most long-range airlines seem to have adopted it — particularly if their routes involve long duty periods through difficult time-zone changes. Certainly some form of rest-area is needed on these flights, and the only real alternative to the attic is an old-style 'Portakabin' type room at the rear of the passenger deck — which worked well enough on earlier 747s, but it took up valuable space that would otherwise be used for revenue-earning seats. The attic can now be retrofitted to most early 747s (including the 100, 200, and 300-series aircraft), but not to Combi variants because the installation would interfere with the handling of cargo containers.

LEFT: Artist's impression and graphic of the flightdeck and crew rest area showing seating arrangement. *Boeing*

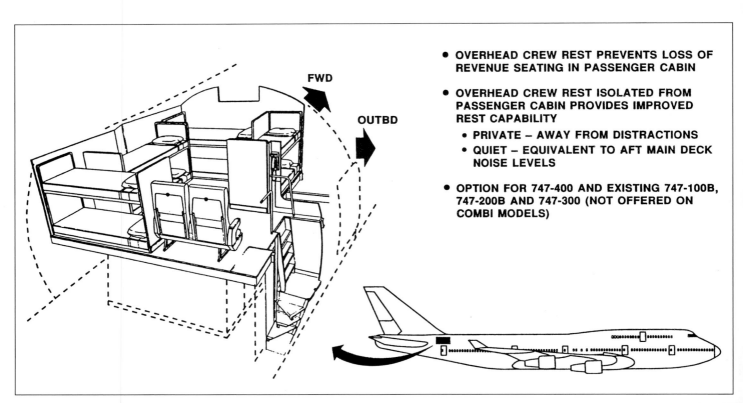

- OVERHEAD CREW REST PREVENTS LOSS OF REVENUE SEATING IN PASSENGER CABIN

- OVERHEAD CREW REST ISOLATED FROM PASSENGER CABIN PROVIDES IMPROVED REST CAPABILITY
  - PRIVATE – AWAY FROM DISTRACTIONS
  - QUIET – EQUIVALENT TO AFT MAIN DECK NOISE LEVELS

- OPTION FOR 747-400 AND EXISTING 747-100B, 747-200B AND 747-300 (NOT OFFERED ON COMBI MODELS)

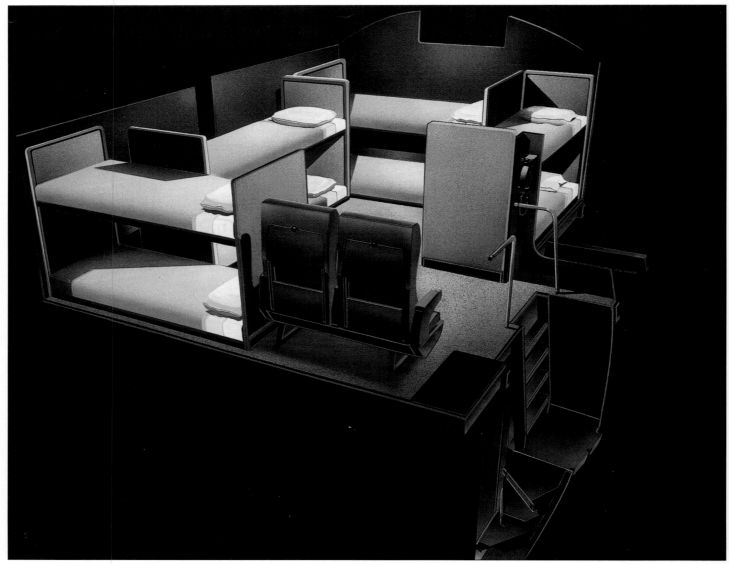

PASSENGER CABINS

The 747-400 is based on an internally modified fuselage and stretched upper deck of the 747-300. Most of the passenger facilities and systems have been upgraded in some way, and a great deal of work has gone into the improvement of cabin flexibility. The nose-to-tail re-design effort was forced to start with an underlying structure that was already more than twenty years old: this imposed a number of restrictions, but it also had the huge advantage that the study was able to draw on lessons accumulated during countless hours of airline service. Many new ideas were incorporated to reduce both daily and long-term maintenance costs, and experienced operators were given a very real influence over the final design changes. Most operators, for example, reported problems of one sort or another with 747 main-deck floor panels: in some cases these had been caused by poor protection against corrosion, and in others by stress delamination of the bonded aluminium/PVC panels. As a result of this consultation process, the new 747 was designed with much tougher graphite based materials in the panels themselves, and an impermeable damp course-style barrier was installed around all potentially wet areas such as toilets and galleys: the floor panels were also fixed in place by liquid-sealed fasteners, which prevented any fluids seeping through to the supporting structure. Under the main passenger deck — in all the cargo and equipment bays — every exposed surface was protected by a white epoxy coating, which completely sealed the internal structure, and gave early warning of potential problems by highlighting the slightest signs of staining.

The passenger compartments of the 400-series are exactly the same size as those of the earlier 747-300, but new layouts and better materials have resulted in more flexibility and a completely new appearance. The overhead luggage bins have been enlarged, and all the ceiling lights have been concealed to give a much softer, 'skylight' effect: this combination has cleverly created the illusion of an even wider main deck than the original. New fabrics and warmer colours have somehow managed to give a more homely and welcoming look to the vast acres of cabin space. The inner face of the contoured wall panels was subtly changed to make them easier to clean, and the 'engineering' side was provided with improved fixings to make them less troublesome to remove and install during a major service. New and much more stringent fire, smoke and toxicity regulations were introduced in the late-1980s, and these made it necessary to change most of the existing cabin materials. All polycarbonates were replaced by a chemically blended thermoplastic compound, and graphite or phenolic plastics were used in place of conventional epoxy-glassfibre.

The centreline galley and toilet units on the 747-400 are all located on structural hardpoints, complete with plumbing and electrical connections, and fully sealed against all liquid based

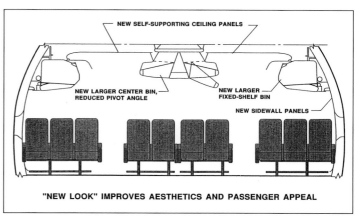

"NEW LOOK" IMPROVES AESTHETICS AND PASSENGER APPEAL

LEFT: Cabin crew rest area — the so-called 'attic' bedroom — is located directly beneath the leading edge of the fin. Not available on the Combi the number of bunks and seats is optional. *Boeing*

RIGHT: Interior architecture of the 747-400 showing redesigned overhead luggage bins. *Boeing*

LEFT: Interior architecture of the 747-400 showing the skylight-effect concealed lighting and redesigned overhead luggage bins. *Boeing*

RIGHT: Various examples of seating plans showing the versatility of the 747-400's vast cabins. *Boeing*

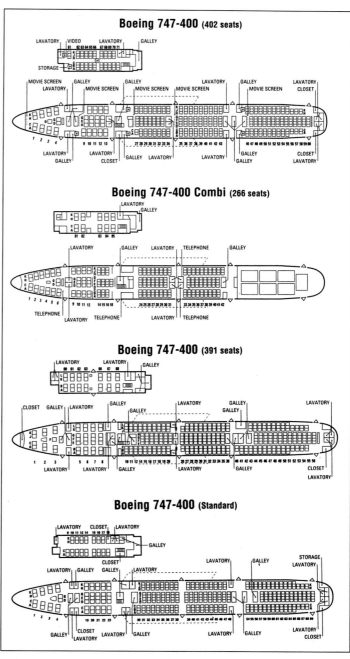

corrosive elements. The outboard units have been designed with maximum flexibility of cabin arrangements in mind: they are all modular in construction and virtually self-contained, and can be moved to a new position simply by locking them into the normal seat-track system. There are more than 150 potential galley and toilet locations included on the basic aircraft plan, but only about 25 of these will be completed with appropriate pipework and wiring as part of the initial hull price — others can be incorporated as an option, but at extra cost.

The modular lavatory units on the 747-400 have been substantially upgraded, and now operate on the vacuum-flushing principle. This is a huge advance on the gravity-flush system of all previous versions of the aircraft, and goes a long way to making the units completely odour free. The whole layout of the toilet system is designed to enable each zone of the passenger cabin to be served by at least two of the four separate vacuum-tanks at the rear of the aircraft: this means that any single system-failure will not cause too much disruption. At the end of each flight, all four tanks can be emptied at once through a single-point service panel.

To accommodate the change of cabin configuration, many of the overhead luggage bins can now be moved. The associated passenger-service units (with fresh air vent, staff call button and reading lamp) can also be movable, or, if the customer wishes, fixed in one position and capable of serving several different seat configurations.

747 SEATING ARRANGEMENTS

With such a range of flight length options there is also a wide choice in passenger numbers and seating. The following details show how individual airlines have arranged their 747-400 accommodation in different ways.

Generally each airline uses exactly the same internal layout but it is noticeable that some airlines — for example, JAL, Qantas, SIA, etc — use different configurations for different routes, reflecting the carrier's past experience of ticket sales and the length of the route involved. The following details show how individual airlines have different seating arrangements for their 747-400s.

AIR CANADA	747-433 Combi	
Executive Class	43	
Hospitality Class	253	
Total seating	296 (Plus 7 freight containers)	

AIR FRANCE	747-428	747-428 Combi
L'Espace 180	13	13
L'Espace 127	56	56
Tempo	321	181
Total seating	390	250 *

*Plus 7 freight containers

ALL NIPPON AIRWAYS 747-481*		
*Two configurations		
First Class	19	19
Club Class	83	62
Economy	220	260
Total seating	322	341

BRITISH AIRWAYS	747-436
First Class	18
Club World	55
World Traveller	340
Total seating	413

CANADIAN AIRWAYS INTERNATIONAL   747-475

Business Class	48
Canadian Class	379
Total seating	427

CATHAY PACIFIC AIRWAYS   747-467

First Class	18
Business Class	67
Economy	313
Total seating	398

CHINA AIRLINES   747-409

First Class	18
Business Class	93
Economy	316
Total seating	427

GARUDA INDONESIAN AIRWAYS 747-4U3

First Class	18
Executive Class	62
Economy	323
Total seating	403

JAPAN AIRLINES   747-446*
*Three configurations)

First Class	19	19	19
JAL Executive	157	76	30
Economy	128	278	353
Total seating	304	373	402

LUFTHANSA   747-430*   **747-430 Combi**
*Two configurations

First Class	20	20	20
Busines Class	96	51	51
Economy	252	322	195
Total seating	368	393	266*

*Plus 7 freight containers)

QANTAS   747-438*
*Two configurations

Luxury First Class	10	16
Business Class	50	65
Economy	330	291
Total seating	390	372

SINGAPORE AIRLINES 747-412*
*Two configurations

First Class	24	16
Business Class	53	65
Economy	316	316
Total seating	393	397

SOUTH AFRICAN AIRWAYS 747-444

First Class	18
Business Class	66
Economy	263
Total seating	347

THAI AIRWAYS INTERNATIONAL   747-4D7

Royal First Class	18
Royal Executive Class	62
Economy	332
Total seating	412

UNITED AIRLINES   747-422

First Class	18
Connoisseur Class	80
Economy	320
Total seating	418

VIRGIN ATLANTIC   747-4Q8

Upper Class	48
Premium Economy Class	22
Economy	340
Total seating	410

AIR CONDITIONING SYSTEM

In the absence of a flight engineer, air conditioning, pressurisation and temperature control on the 747-400 has become a fully automated, set-and-forget operation, with automatic utilisation of back-up systems where necessary. The aircraft has three identical air conditioning packs, plus four filtered re-circulation fans, to ensure a constant ventilation rate throughout the various passenger-cabin zones: the temperature of each zone can be pre-selected, and adjusted independently. The main passenger cabin — including the staff rest-area — is now divided up into five individual air-conditioning zones (compared with just three on all earlier 747 models), with the flightdeck and upper passenger-cabin treated as two separate and additional zones. The whole system now operates at a much higher ventilation rate, and digital sensing has allowed more precise control of both temperature and humidity.

To the great relief of all pilots, the purser's station in the passenger cabin now includes a simplified control panel, which enables the cabin crew to adjust the temperature of each zone independently. Cabin altitude (pressurisation) is controlled by regulating the discharge of 'used' air through two outflow valves at the rear of the aircraft. All normal functions of air-conditioning operation are controlled automatically, but manual reversion is available if necessary. The FMC now sends the altitude of the destination-airfield to the pressurisation system, which ensures that the gradual depressurisation from cruise altitude to landing altitude is handled smoothly and progressively.

PERFORMANCE IMPROVEMENT PACKAGE

In April 1993 Boeing announced a series of minor aerodynamic and operating changes to the baseline 747-400, to be followed by a major structural upgrade, which together formed the so-called Performance Improvement Package (PIP). These overall changes represented a two-stage effort to provide a more efficient aeroplane, with more range and a significantly improved take-off weight: the first phase was being made available almost immediately, and the second planned for approval in mid-1996.

The first stage of this programme centred on several detail improvements to the existing airframe: these were due to be incorporated on all production aircraft built after mid-1993, and were offered as retrofit kits for all earlier 747-400s. The package included a re-designed dorsal fairing, which was manufactured in composite materials rather than the original aluminium: this was attached to the lower leading edge of the fin, increasing its chord and improving the airflow over the fin/fuselage junction. The original PIP plan included a revised fuel-transfer system from the horizontal stabiliser tank to the centre wing tank: this had always been a simple on-demand system which automatically allowed the fuel to flow down as the centre tank emptied. The revised scheme delayed this transfer, keeping the weight of the tail fuel behind the centre-of-gravity for as long as possible — thus improving the trim-drag of the aircraft, and reducing its overall fuel burn. The system was extensively flight-tested, but it was finally dropped from the programme because the actual benefits did not justify the planned changes. The third element of the package involved re-rigging the wing-mounted spoilers. Operational experience had found that these surfaces tended to lift away from the wing slightly in the cruise because of their position in an area of low aerodynamic pressure: this caused turbulence over the upper wing surface and generated unnecessary drag. The solution was to hold the spoiler panels down under much higher load. All three major elements of the first phase of the PIP were tested together on a factory-fresh United Airlines aircraft (believed to be N190UA), which was specially leased by Boeing to conduct a series of long-endurance flights. Performance details later released by Seattle showed that the dorsal fairing and spoiler changes alone, would improve the overall drag of the 747-400 by at least 0.5 percent — which seems a fairly insignificant figure, but in today's terms this represents a fuel saving of some $75-100,000 per aircraft per year.

While the PIP flight testing was in progress, Boeing completed an extended structural audit of the 747-400, to provide the certification authorities with a case for increasing the gross take-off weight to 875,000lb (397,000kg). The new weight had been specifically requested by the Australian carrier Qantas, to allow more payload to be carried on critical sectors such as Los Angeles–Sydney and Singapore–London. Qantas had previously been operating its aircraft up to the maximum available limit of 870,000lb (394,500kg), but the new weight (which was introduced on scheduled services from the end of November 1993) allowed up to an extra 15 passengers on the 6,500nm (12,050km) Los

Angeles–Sydney route. Although Qantas pioneered the new limit, and worked closely with Boeing to achieve certification, it was immediately made available to other airlines and quickly became the new upper limit.

The second phase of the Performance Improvement Package was a great deal more ambitious, and could have seen the maximum take-off weight rise to 932,000lb (422,700kg), and the range increase to around 8,000nm (14,800km). It would have required considerable structural changes, including heavier gauge wing skins; a stronger centre-section carry-through box; a beefed-up undercarriage, and increased fuel tankage: new operating procedures and autopilot software would also have been needed. The big advantage of this scheme was that it would have provided an ideal stepping-stone into the long awaited fuselage stretch, which might have added another 80 passenger seats to a typical airline load-sheet. As it turned out, this project coincided with yet another big recession in the air transport industry, and no progress has yet been made on this or several other schemes to stretch the 747.

BELOW: With such large numbers of passengers aboard, the 747-400 cabin crew needs to be able to evacuate the aircraft speedily. This drawing shows the escape slides from the aircraft and areas lit by exterior lights. *Boeing*

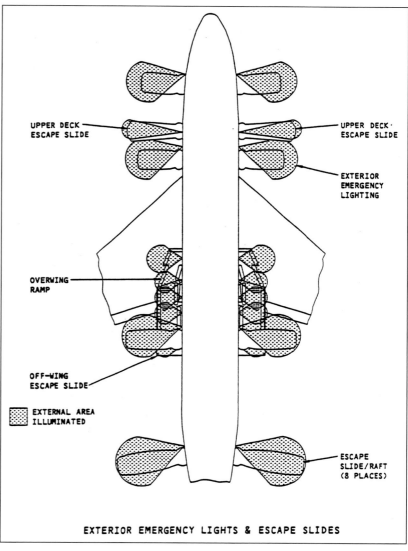

UPPER DECK ESCAPE SLIDE

UPPER DECK ESCAPE SLIDE

EXTERIOR EMERGENCY LIGHTING

OVERWING RAMP

OFF-WING ESCAPE SLIDE

EXTERNAL AREA ILLUMINATED

ESCAPE SLIDE/RAFT (8 PLACES)

EXTERIOR EMERGENCY LIGHTS & ESCAPE SLIDES

5 IN SERVICE

747-400: THE BASELINE PASSENGER VERSION

The passenger version of the 747-400 is the foundation stone of the whole programme, and currently represents nearly 85 percent of all the aircraft in service. The first aircraft to fly was powered by Pratt & Whitney PW4056 engines, and was given a specially-reserved descriptive registration (N401PW) for the first flight on 29 April 1988, and for the duration of the subsequent FAA certification programme. The aircraft was fully refurbished after its period of test flying, and finally handed over to Northwest Airlines as N661US on 8 December 1989. Other aircraft used in the certification programme included the first General Electric CF6-powered example (N5573S — later handed over to Lufthansa as D-ABVB); and the first with Rolls-Royce RB211 engines (N1788B), which was eventually delivered to Cathay Pacific as VR-HOO. The first 747-400 delivery to a customer was N663US, which was handed over to Northwest Airlines on 26 January 1989.

The original maximum take-off weight of the 747-400 series was 870,000lb (394,500kg), but this has now been increased to an optional 875,000lb (397,000kg) — and may soon go even higher. Airline seating plans vary considerably, but a typical example might include around 420 seats, in three classes. Most airlines — though certainly not all — use the forward-section of the lower deck for First Class, luxury seating; the upper deck for 'Club Class' (or equivalent), and the centre and rear sections of the lower deck for 10-abreast Tourist Class accommodation — generally in 3–4–3 configuration. At the present time (March 1998), nearly 350 all-passenger models have been delivered to more than 30 airlines.

747-400 COMBI: THE PASSENGER/CARGO CARRIER

The name Combi is derived from the combination of passenger and cargo loads on the same deck. The very first 747 Combi was actually a re-manufactured 100-series aircraft (OO-SGA), which was the first of a pair converted from standard passenger-carrying models for the Belgian airline Sabena. The work was done by Boeing during the slack winter period of 1973/74, and the aircraft was returned to Brussels in February 1974. The new sub-type was an immediate success and attracted many other buyers — not just as a conversion programme, but as a factory-prepared option.

The first Combi manufactured at Everett as a wholly new aircraft was C-GAGA, a 747-200B Combi, built for Air Canada and delivered at the end of March 1975. The new

ABOVE RIGHT: The baseline passenger 747-400: Virgin Atlantic's G-VFAB *Lady Penelope. Rob Holder*

RIGHT: The Combi, passenger/cargo carrying 747-400: KLM Asia's PH-BFC at Schiphol in August 1997. *Gerry Manning*

BELOW: Upper deck comparison between 747-100/200 and 747-300/-400. *Boeing*

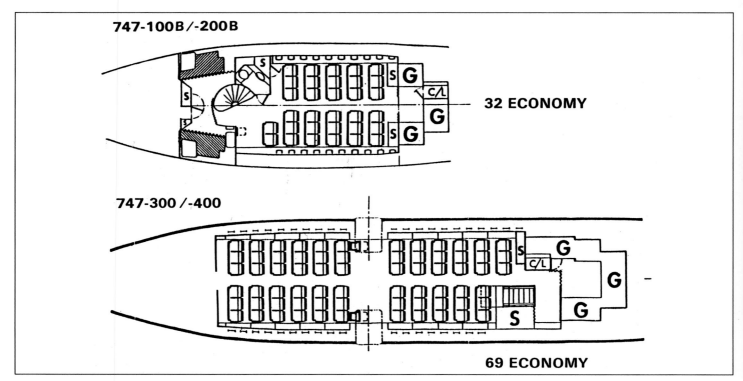

747-100B/-200B

32 ECONOMY

747-300/-400

69 ECONOMY

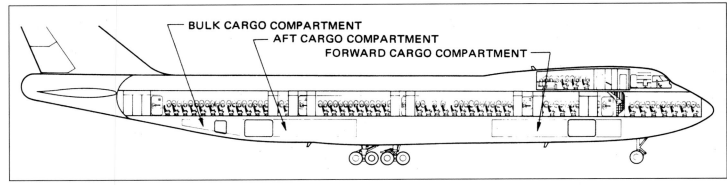

BULK CARGO COMPARTMENT
AFT CARGO COMPARTMENT
FORWARD CARGO COMPARTMENT

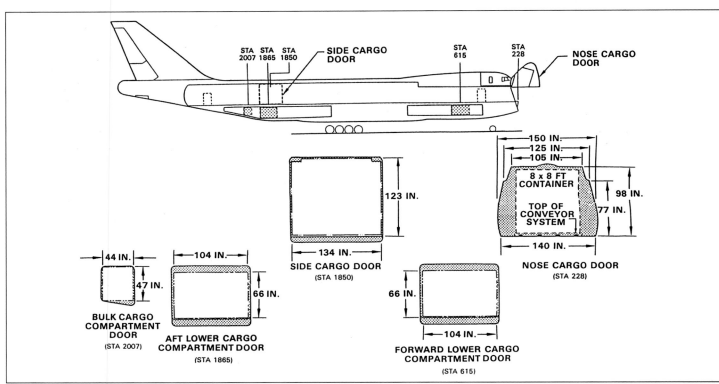

STA 2007 STA 1865 STA 1850   SIDE CARGO DOOR   STA 615   STA 228   NOSE CARGO DOOR

123 IN.
134 IN.
SIDE CARGO DOOR
(STA 1850)

150 IN.
125 IN.
105 IN.
8 x 8 FT CONTAINER
TOP OF CONVEYOR SYSTEM
98 IN.
77 IN.
140 IN.
NOSE CARGO DOOR
(STA 228)

44 IN.
47 IN.
BULK CARGO COMPARTMENT DOOR
(STA 2007)

104 IN.
66 IN.
AFT LOWER CARGO COMPARTMENT DOOR
(STA 1865)

66 IN.
104 IN.
FORWARD LOWER CARGO COMPARTMENT DOOR
(STA 615)

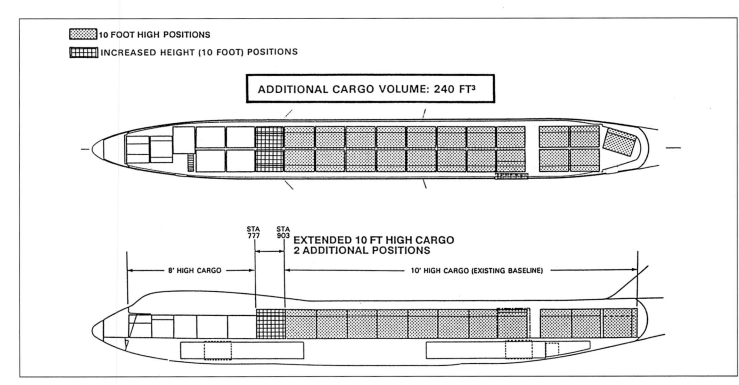

10 FOOT HIGH POSITIONS

INCREASED HEIGHT (10 FOOT) POSITIONS

ADDITIONAL CARGO VOLUME: 240 FT³

STA 777 STA 903   EXTENDED 10 FT HIGH CARGO 2 ADDITIONAL POSITIONS

8' HIGH CARGO   10' HIGH CARGO (EXISTING BASELINE)

model was fitted with a 120in (305cm) high by 134in (340cm) wide, upwards opening cargo-door on the port side of the rear fuselage: it also had a strengthened floor in the rear of the main deck, and a roller-conveyor system to allow larger cargo containers to be moved around and locked into position.

The forward passenger compartment was separated from the cargo deck by a removable internal bulkhead, which allowed each airline to choose its own mix of passenger and cargo accommodation. The great flexibility of the Combi concept quickly established it as one of Boeing's most popular 747 models. Apart from its stretched upper deck and updated internal systems, the 747-400 fuselage is virtually unchanged from the original 100/200-series, so all the trappings of Combi operation have now been directly transferred to the new generation of digital aircraft.

The first 400-series Combi (PH-BFC and PH-BFD) were both delivered to KLM in September 1989, and since then more than 30 have been completed for nine different carriers. However, it has to be said that the 747 Combi is not quite so popular now as it once was — perhaps because ETOPS certifications have made it possible to use smaller-capacity, twin-engined aircraft on transatlantic routes, which makes the availability of 'spare' capacity less likely.

Combis retain all the windows of a passenger version, and are usually fitted with hardened flooring in the rear fuselage for a basic six or 12-pallet cargo load: in each case an optional (7th or 13th) pallet can be carried in the tapered area beneath the tail of the aircraft, but this needs additional loading and tie-down facilities. A typical 6/7-pallet aircraft can also seat up to 268 passengers in the forward section of the main deck and the upper deck: with all the pallet-handling equipment removed, the cabin can be returned to full all-passenger configuration, and its capacity restored to around 420 seats.

747-400F: THE GLOBAL CARGO CARRIER

Compared with a conventional 200-series freighter, the new 747-400F carries about 20 percent more payload over ranges that are more than 1,000nm longer. The aircraft was an obvious addition to the new model range, but it was developed as a significantly different aeroplane to the original passenger version. The 747-400F still has all the modern efficiency of the upgraded systems and two-crew flightdeck; the longer span wing and winglets; the new Pratt & Whitney auxiliary power unit; the carbon brakes and tail mounted fuel tank; but it does not have the extended upper deck of the passenger and Combi versions, nor does the fuselage have any windows or passenger entrance/exit doors.

TOP LEFT: The lower hold compartment of the 747-400 is modelled on that of the 747-200 series. *Boeing*

ABOVE LEFT AND LEFT: Plan and side views of the 747-400F showing cargo door arrangements and how the absence of the extended upper deck adds to the number of 120in (305cm) high container positions. *Boeing*

The aircraft has all the outward appearance of a 200-series which has been fitted with the extended wing and winglets. The upper deck of any 747 has always been considered something of a nuisance by cargo operators: access to it from the main cargo deck is normally available only via a trap-door and vertical ladder, and the conventional passenger escape doors are far too small to allow the loading of any useful cargo — the whole area is generally thought to be wasted space. The floor of the upper deck also intrudes into the lower deck roof space — reducing its effective ceiling height by at least two feet, and limiting the vertical size of containers that will pass underneath it.

The nose of the specialist cargo aircraft is fine for very long loads, but will not allow anything taller than 8ft to pass beneath the cockpit floor and through into the main deck space beyond. The ceiling of the rear compartment is much higher, and the upwards-opening side cargo door will allow the traditional 10ft high road/rail container to pass through with ease. Using a powered roller-conveyor system built into the aircraft floor, these big containers can be manoeuvred inside the fuselage and locked into position both side-by-side and nose-to-tail, to form two complete rows. If the stretched upper deck had been included in the 747-400F, its intrusive floor would have forced the cargo operators to use 8ft high containers in the forward fuselage, In terms of volume, the main deck of the 747-400F has 21,547cu ft (603cu m) of cargo space, and the lower hold (which is normally used on a passenger aircraft for containerised baggage) an additional 4,013cu ft (112cu m).

The maximum payload weight for the 400-series is 243,000lb (110,000kg). The non-stop range of the 747-400F with full payload is now quoted as 4,400nm (8,100km), which has enabled several carriers to open up brand new routes, or even revitalise their profit-potential on existing routes. Cargolux for example, recently claimed that the 400-series aircraft saves them more than 300 refuelling stops per year — each one costing about $15,000 for the additional fuel used during the descent from cruise altitude; the airport landing and parking fees; the extra crew time involved, and the climb back up to cruise altitude.

Despite its remarkable performance, sales of the 747-400F have been considerably less than Boeing anticipated. Plans for the aircraft were first announced in the summer of 1988, and Air France placed an order for five about a year later: these were subsequently cancelled in favour of the Combi version, and Cargolux actually became the first operator of the type when it took delivery of one of the cancelled Air France aeroplanes in May 1993. Since then, the Cargolux fleet has been expanded to five with their own orders, and several other airlines have joined the elite band of all-cargo operators (see the production list). The biggest potential operator of the 747-400F is Colorado-based US cargo carrier Atlas Air — which in June 1997 signed a $1.7billion contract for 10 firm orders for CF6-80C2 powered aircraft, plus 10 optional delivery positions: the first four aircraft are due for delivery during 1998, and the remaining six will follow between 1999 and 2001.

747-400D: THE DOMESTIC PEOPLE-CARRIER

The third individual model of the 747-400 is the highly specialised 'domestic' aircraft — much used by the two major Japanese carriers. This is an upgraded version of the old SR (Short Range) concept, which was first developed in the early 1970s to cope with the high-capacity shuttle-type operations between the major island groups of Japan. The 400D has the extended upper deck and two-crew cockpit of a conventional 400-series fuselage, but the longer wing and upturned winglets have been omitted. From the outside therefore, this aircraft looks almost exactly the same as a 747-300: the only clues to its real identity are the slight difference in appearance of the low-profile tyres, and the subtle aerodynamic changes to the engine-pylons and wing/fuselage intersection.

Internally the aircraft is a standard 747-400, but without the optional long-range facilities such as the flightdeck bedroom, the cabin-crew rest area and the extra fuel tank in the horizontal tail. The full aerodynamic advantages of the longer-span wing and new winglets of the conventional 747-400 only become apparent during very long periods of high-altitude cruising flight. With an average flight time of less than 60 minutes, the 'domestic' aircraft spends a very high proportion of its time either climbing to, or descending from, what might be called a normal cruise altitude. Under these circumstances, it was obviously pointless to carry the extra weight of the new wing structures if no benefit could be gained from their inclusion. It was therefore decided to use a near-conventional 747 wing design, but to manufacture it using all the new alloys, and make provision for later modification to full 747-400 standard. In this way, the aircraft could fly all the arduous short-range sectors — with their punishing regime of frequent landings and take-offs — during the early part of its operational life, and then go back into the workshops to have the wing-tips and other long-range equipment installed.

With the full 747-400 specification restored, the aircraft could then return to service on the kind of long-endurance flights it was designed for. This long-term operating technique gives an improved overall fatigue life — both by limiting the total number of take-off/touchdown cycles, and by reducing the number of landings per flying hour. The 400D wing was manufactured with all the conversion fixings already in place, and at least one aircraft (JA8955 — operated by All Nippon) has now been fitted with its full wing extensions and returned to normal 747-style operations. Because all journey times around the Japanese islands are very short, the passenger cabins of the 747-400D are configured more like a bus or tube train than a typical airliner. No less than 624 passengers can be carried in these high-density seating arrangements, compared with about 420 in a conventional three-class layout, and 496 in just two classes: day-to-day galley facilities are also somewhat limited. The short range and domestic models were specially developed for a very particular niche market, and Japan has consistently remained the only buyer — with All Nippon Airways currently operating 11 of the 400-series, and Japan Airlines eight.

C-33: THE MILITARY FREIGHTER PROPOSAL

During 1995 Boeing offered a military cargo version of the 747-400F to the US Air Force, under the designation C-33. This proposal was designed to meet the requirements of the Non-Developmental Airlift Aircraft (NDAA) programme, at a time when the Department of Defense was seeking a much cheaper alternative to further batches of the McDonnell-Douglas C-17 Globemaster II. The 'non-developmental' part of this programme insisted that the aircraft concerned should be totally 'off the shelf', and not in need of any further development work. The bid was eventually unsuccessful, and presumably will not now be repeated (because Boeing now owns the C-17 programme).

YAL-1A: THE LASER-ATTACK AIRCRAFT

A modified version of the Boeing 747-400F has been selected by the US Air Force to carry an airborne attack-laser system, designed to shoot down short/medium-range ballistic missiles during their early boost phase. The system is based on a chemical oxygen-iodine laser (COIL), which will occupy a steerable turret in the nose. If all goes well, the COIL should have a range of between 160-320nm (300-600km), and be capable of up to 30 firings without recharging. The programme suggests that a standard 747-400F will be taken from the production line in 1999 and flown down to Boeing's Wichita plant for modification.

Flight testing will begin in 2002, by which time a second demonstrator will be well on the way to completion. After allowing for a period of full weapons-system testing (live-firing against real missiles) and development, a final go-ahead decision should be possible in FY2005. Five more aircraft will then be built to production standards, making seven in all. The first three should reach initial operating capability in the latter part of FY2006, and all seven should achieve full operational status by FY2008: the two development prototypes will be brought up to production standards once the full weapons-system configuration is known. The operational squadron will mount standing patrols over friendly territory at about 40,000ft (12,200m), giving each laser between 40-60 seconds to find, identify and shoot-down each target. Major concerns at the moment appear to be adequate power-generation on board the aircraft (the standard 747 has only four 90kVa generators), and providing workable aerodynamics around the big rotating nose-turret.

ABOVE RIGHT: The global cargo carrier: Singapore Airlines is one of the world's major operators of cargo aircraft with six 747-412Fs and another on order. *Geoff Harber*

RIGHT: The domestic people carrier: a computer enhanced photograph showing a 747-400D: note absence of winglets and shorter wing. In appearance very similar to the 747-300, it has the two-man cockpit, and all the other 747-400 attributes. *Boeing*

747-500X AND 747-600X

These two projects first emerged as serious contenders in 1995, and nearly became a reality when they were announced at the 1996 Farnborough Airshow. The -500X was planned as a modest 19ft 6in (6m) stretch of the basic 747-400, with three-class accommodation for about 530 passengers or high-density seating for at least 600: the target range of the aircraft was more than 7,000nm (12,950km). The much bigger -600X was a 59ft 6in (18m) stretched version of the existing fuselage, which was designed for 650-800 seats. It later emerged that both of these projects would be fitted with a new wing — possibly up to 259ft 1in (79m) span — which was based on the aft-loaded aerodynamics of the Boeing 777: winglets were not included, but the wing/body centre-section was completely new. By this time, the proposed range of the -500 was 9,200nm (14,800km), and that of the -600 was 7,000nm (12,950km).

Over the following six months a confusing and often contradictory array of capacities, weights and performance details were released, but little hard evidence of commitment emerged — either from Boeing or from the airlines. All three engine manufacturers were asked to submit proposals, and derivatives of the PW4168, GE CF6-80E1 and RR Trent 800 were all 'floated' as possibilities. In May 1996 Boeing announced that fly-by-wire technology would be used on the new aircraft — but only for the trailing-edge flaps: the ailerons, spoilers and rudder would all have conventional control systems. Most of the airlines wanted full FBW, and as much commonalty with the Boeing 777 as possible. Take-off weights in the order of 1,130,000lb (513,000kg) were now being discussed, which would need a brand-new six-wheel undercarriage on the pouter trucks, and a four-wheel nose-gear.

By this time technology and ambition were beginning to run away with the project, and the first signs of dissent were being expressed: airport managers were uneasy about the 279ft (85m) length of the fuselage, and air traffic control authorities were concerned about the wake-turbulence of such a heavy aircraft. Worst of all perhaps, potential customers were beginning to baulk at the price of these two machines — up to $230 million for the -600X, and only a little less for the smaller -500X. Both new models were formally announced at Farnborough in September 1996, and although several airlines had expressed considerable interest, none was willing to fully commit themselves: the price had become a major stumbling block — especially in the middle of the significant recession that was threatening south-east Asia. United Airlines and Malaysian Airlines were 'almost reconciled' to an early order, followed perhaps by British Airways, Singapore Airlines, Thai Airways and Cathay Pacific — but none of them actually got around to signing a firm contract. In December 1996, Boeing announced a six-month delay in the 747-500/600X programmes — caused apparently by continuing market uncertainty — and in January even Ron Woodward, the president of Boeing's Commercial Airplane Group, expressed some misgivings about the programme. Later that month Seattle announced that they had decided to drop the 747-500/600 programmes in favour of longer-range, high-capacity variants of the 777. The planned development of the 747 was going to cost about $7 billion, and the commercial case for it was getting weaker every day.

747-400IGW: A SIMPLER UPGRADE

After shelving the 747-500/600X models, Boeing returned to the idea of a considerably less dramatic development of the basic 747-400 — concentrating on relatively modest weight and capacity improvements. A whole raft of ideas have been discussed under the general description 747-400IGW (Increased Gross Weight) — some of them becoming quite complicated from an engineering point of view, and probably far too risky in the current financial climate.

At the present time Boeing seems to favour the low-risk strategy of fitting a slightly strengthened 747-400F wing and undercarriage to an updated version of the original 747-200 fuselage. The removal of the stretched upper deck would save about 8,800lb (4,000kg) of structural weight, at the cost of 30-40 passenger seats. The big advantage of this scheme would be the stronger wing, which would allow the gross take-off weight to rise (as an option) to 910,000lb (413,000kg): additional belly fuel tanks would bring the range of this 355-380 seater up to well beyond the 8,000nm (14,800km) mark. Any further increase in gross weight would almost certainly require major changes to the wing, undercarriage, and both elements of the tail: power requirements for the 910,000lb (413,636kg) aircraft could be handled by derivatives of today's engines, but further increases in weight would probably need something much bigger.

At the present time (March 1998) this aircraft is being called the 747-200ERX — the ERX suffix representing Extended Range — but it seems likely that the model number will be changed at some time in the future, to reflect the aircraft's status as an offshoot of the 747-400 programme. The Taiwanese carrier EVA Airways has already expressed a strong interest in the 200ERX to operate its direct Taipei/US East Coast services.

IN-FLIGHT ENTERTAINMENT

As with all other long-haul manufacturers, Boeing has been looking hard at interactive in-seat video systems as well as individual video systems. The aviation press in June 1994 announced that BE Aerospace, a Florida-based company, had won the contest to supply British Airways' fleet requirements. The winning system, the B/E 4000 multi-media digital distribution system, was due to be installed in BA's 747s and 767s in early 1995. It was to provide up to 24 video channels, interactive games, pay-per-view channels, shopping, telephone, etc. In-seat video orders were also gained by BEA from Canada, USAir, EVA Air and Philippine Airlines.

The trouble was that it just didn't work efficiently enough. British Airways chief operating officer Alistair Cummings would be quoted in late 1997 saying, 'Two years ago airlines looked ahead to the new era of in-flight entertainment, but something has gone seriously wrong and we have come down to earth with a bump.' By December 1997, the party was over. BA dropped BEA and announced a tie-up with

Hughes-Aviecom, despite good reports of the non-interactive version of the BEA system from Asiana and JAL. Qantas was to follow suit and plump for Hughes in early 1998.

British Airways was not the only airline suffering from in-flight entertainment reliability problems: the interactive elements of Cathay Pacific's Matsushita's System 2000E were cut back because of reliability; Virgin Atlantic's Hughes-Avicom hardware suffered setbacks, although improvements came with the Odyssey. On the other hand SIA, which also uses the Matsushita platform, is pleased with the results, although it has had to increase the maintenance teams substantially following in-flight entertainment's launch. Most recent airline to drop interactivity was Qantas in July 1997.

There's another problem with IFE: the problem of the seats theselves; no longer designed purely for comfort, they now have to be electronics platforms. This increases their weight and therefore the stress on the flooring, especially when involved on dynamic testing. If the new 16g test were to be applied retrospectively to older aircraft built in the days of a 9g requirement, the 747 fleet would be very vulnerable. On top of the weight, the dissipation of all the heat generated can also cause problems.

There's no doubt that IFE has a long way to go before complete interactive systems are in place and working well — but the current in-seat video systems are certainly better than the old one-screen per cabin system.

BELOW AND RIGHT: General arrangement views and size comparisons of Boeing's 747-500X/-600X. *Boeing*

OVERLEAF: A Boeing impression of what the huge 747-500X/-600X would look like in comparison with the -400. Note lack of winglets. *Boeing*

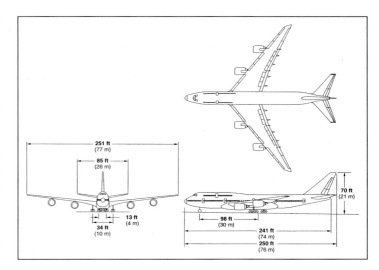

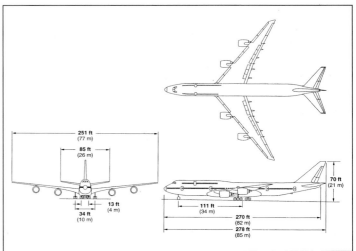

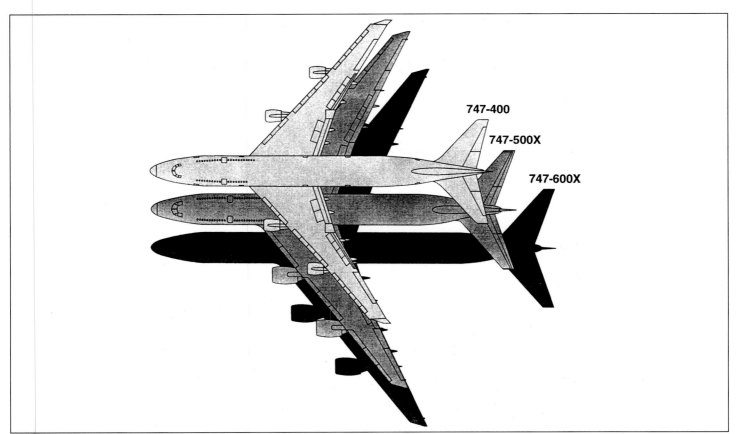

BOEING

747-400

19.41 m
(63 ft 8 in)

70.66 m
(231 ft 10 in)

747-500X

21 m
(70 ft)

76 m
(250 ft)

747-600X

21 m
(70 ft)

85.0 m
(279 ft)

BOEING 747-400

747-400

747-500X

747-600X

	747-400	747-500X	747-600X
Passengers	416	462	548
Range	7,300 nmi 13,520 km (8,400 miles)	8,700 nmi 16,100 km (10,000 miles)	7,750 nmi 14,350 km (8,900 miles)
Engines	PW4056 CF6-80C2 RB211-524G	The 747-500/600 would employ Rolls-Royce RB211-Trent 976 or GE/Pratt & Whitney JV1 producing 68,000-70,000 lb thrust for the 747-500X, and 76,000-78,000 lb thrust for the 747-600X	
Max Takeoff Weight	396,890 kg (875,000 lb)	528,900 kg (1,166,000 lb)	538,000 kg (1,186,000 lb)
Cruising Altitude	12,500 m (41,000 ft)	same	same
Cruising Speed	Mach 0.85 (600+ mph)	same	same
City Pairs	London-Tokyo Singapore-London Los Angeles-Sydney	Jakarta-Amsterdam Johannesburg-New York LAX-Sydney w/cargo Detroit- Hong Kong New York-Hong Kong	Tokyo-London Singapore-London Los Angeles-Hong Kong New York-Tokyo

(Figures for the 747-500X and 747-600X may change subject to firm configuration)

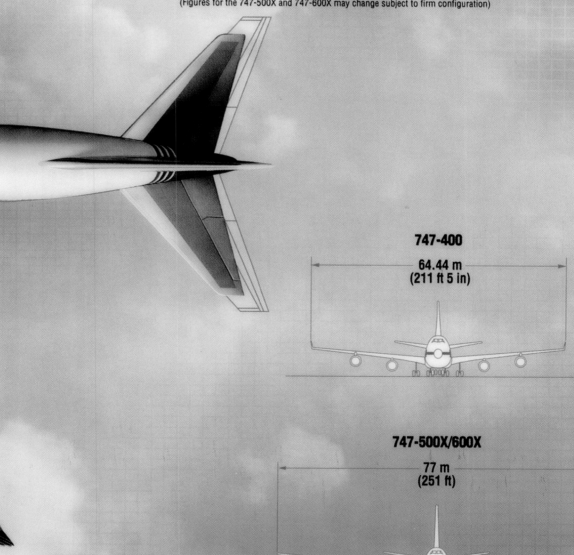

747-400

64.44 m
(211 ft 5 in)

747-500X/600X

77 m
(251 ft)

6 AIRLINE OPERATORS

747-400 CURRENT FLEETS AND ORDERS (Correct to spring 1998)

Airline	First Aircraft	Delivered	No in fleet	On order
Air Canada	C-GAGL	4/6/91	3 Combi	
Air China	B-2456	13/10/89	10 inc 3 Combi	1
Air France	F-GITA	28/2/91	13 inc 5 Combi	
Air India	VT-ESM	4/8/93	6 inc 4 Combi	1
Air New Zealand	ZK-NBS	14/12/89	5	1
All Nippon	JA8094	28/8/90	20 inc 10 Ds	
Asiana	HL7414	1/11/91	12 inc 5 F and 4 Combi	5
British Airways	G-BNLA	30/6/89	38 inc 2BAA	16
Brunei	V8-AL1	17/4/92	1	
Canadian Airlines Int	C-GMWW	11/12/90	4	
Cargolux	LX-FCV	17/11/93	5 F	
Cathay Pacific	VR-HOO	26/9/88	21 inc 2 F	
China Airlines	B-161	8/2/90	10	2
El Al	4X-ELA	27/4/94	3	
EVA	B-16401	10/11/92	13 inc 10 Combi	1
Garuda Indonesia	PK-GSG	14/1/94	3	
Japan Airlines	JA8071	25/1/90	34 inc 8 Ds	16
Japanese Government	JA8091	17/9/91	2	
KLM	PH-BFA	18/5/89	20 inc 13 Combi	
Korean	HL7477	13/6/89	27 inc 3F and 1 Combi	7
Kuwait Airways	9K-ADE	29/11/94	1 Combi	
Lufthansa	D-ABVA	23/5/89	23 inc 8 Combis	7

BELOW: United's N172UA was delivered to the airline on 21 August 1989, the second of over 30 747-422s now flying with United. *Robbie Shaw*

ABOVE RIGHT: JAL is one of the biggest operators of all models of 747 with a fleet total approaching 100. *Geoff Harber*

Airline	First Aircraft	Delivered	No in fleet	On order
Malaysia Airlines	9M-MHM	6/10/89	16 inc 2 Combis	10
Mandarin	B-16801		1	
Northwest	N663US	26/1/89	10	4
Philippine Air Lines	N751PR	21/12/93	4 inc 1 Combi	7
Qantas	VH-OJA	11/8/89	18	3
Royal Air Maroc	CN-RGA	4/10/93	1	
Saudi Arabian Airlines	HZ-AIV		2	3
Singapore	9V-SMB	18/3/89	43 inc 6 F	11
South African	ZS-SAV	19/1/91	4	1
Thai Airways Intern'l	HS-TGH	21/2/90	12	4
United Air Lines	N171UA	30/6/89	32	25
Varig	PP-VPI	31/5/91	0	6
Virgin Atlantic Airways	G-VFAB	28/4/94	5	1

AIR CANADA
The Canadian flag-carrier's existing fleet of three 747-100 series and three 747-200 Combis was joined in June 1991 by C-GAGL, the first of three PW4056-powered 747-400 series Combis. No additional orders have been placed since.

ABOVE: 747-433 C-GAGL in landing configuration. *Gerry Manning*

BELOW: 747-433 C-GAGM with undercarriage doors just closing at the end of the retraction sequence. *Geoff Harber*

RIGHT: Three views of Air China 747-4J6 Combis: B-2456 (ABOVE RIGHT) and B-2460 (RIGHT and BELOW RIGHT). *Gerry Manning (Top); Hugh Newell*

AIR CHINA

Air China was established on 1 July 1988 as the flag carrier of the People's Republic of China. It had operated a mixed fleet of conventional three-man crew 747s (SPs, 200 Combis and a 200F) before B-2456 was delivered in September 1989, as the first in a batch of three 747-400 series Combis.

Delivery of a second batch (this time of five all-passenger models) began in February 1992, and two more aircraft — making 10 in all — arrived in 1997. All of Air China's 400-series are powered by PW4056 engines.

AIR FRANCE

The French government currently holds 95 percent of the shares in Air France, but this will change in the near future as the airline is soon to be semi-privatised — although the government still intends to hold a controlling interest. More then 40 747s of most major models are currently on the fleet list, but lack of investment in the recent past has resulted in only 13 of these (including six Combis) being the more-efficient 400-series.

Union de Transports Aeriens (UTA) ordered two CF6-80-powered 747-400s on 3 July 1983, mainly for scheduled services to former French colonies in Africa. The two aircraft (F-GEXA and F-GEXB) were delivered in September 1989 and July 1991, and went into service alongside the carrier's existing fleet of 747-200 and 747-300 aircraft. At the end of December 1992, however, UTA was absorbed into Air France, and all traces of the original colours were quickly obliterated.

ABOVE: F-GISD, a 747-428 Combi, was delivered in September 1992. *Robbie Shaw*

BELOW: Air France's F-GISC is another Combi: note side cargo door between the two main passenger doors in the rear fuselage. This 1996 photograph was taken at Paris Charles de Gaulle. *Gerry Manning*

AIR INDIA

The Indian flag-carrier was the first all-jet airline, selling the last of its propeller-driven fleet (Lockheed Constellations) in June 1962. It has been operating 747s since the early days of March 1971, and now owns nine -200 series passenger models, two -300 series Combis, and six all-passenger 747-400s, the first of which (VT-ESM) entered service in July 1993.

ABOVE AND BELOW: 747-437s VT-ESN *Tanjore* (ABOVE) and VT-ESM *Konark*. Both were delivered to Air India in 1993. *Rob Holder; Gerry Manning*

AIR NEW ZEALAND

When Air New Zealand started 747-200 operations in 1981, the company (like its near neighbours Qantas) decided to go for Rolls-Royce engines. This loyalty continued for several years, and saw them through the delivery of five 747-200s and the first three of their 747-400s: in 1994, however, the airline leased two ex-Varig 400-series aircraft with General Electric CF6-80 engines. These aircraft have the same engines as Air New Zealand's fleet of Boeing 767s, and it has now been decided that the next 747-400 (ZK-NBV due for delivery during 1998) should also have the American engines.

TOP AND LEFT: Two views of 747-441 ZK-SUI which was leased from ILFC by Air New Zealand on 17 April 1995. It is one of the ex-Varig CF6-80C2-powered aircraft. *Geoff Harber; Gerry Manning*

ABOVE LEFT: ZK-NBU, one of Air New Zealand's Rolls-Royce-powered 747-419s, which was delivered 14 September 1992. Note the difference in engine nacelles with ZK-SUI. *Hugh Newell*

ALL NIPPON AIRWAYS

Until Japanese carriers were partially deregulated last year (1997), All Nippon Airways (ANA) was generally considered to be the dominant player in the domestic market, with Japan Airlines taking the lead on the international stage. That position seems to have been reversed in the post-deregulation period — with ANA now striving to increase its share of the international market, and JAL beginning to seize the initiative on domestic routes. ANA introduced the 747-400 in 1990, taking the passenger and the special domestic model, but with the option of converting the D to long-range configuration — ANA has already converted one of its 747-400D aircraft like this, and others could follow.

ABOVE LEFT: JA8098, a 747-481 delivered to All Nippon in August 1991. *Geoff Harber*

TOP AND LEFT: Two views of JA8094, which was delivered in August 1990. *Geoff Harber; Rob Holder*

ASIANA AIRLINES

South Korea's worsening economic situation has caused substantial losses for Asiana, and its future fleet plans are under review. This could mean the deferral of some of its six outstanding 400-48E orders (at the end of 1997), but a more likely outcome seems to be the deferral of up to 15 planned 777 deliveries — possibly in favour of more 747-400 freighter capacity: although the value of the won continues to plummet against the US$, cargo markets in the region remain buoyant as Korean industry strives to win export orders. The situation is so serious for Asiana, that some analysts are beginning to question its long-term survival.

ABOVE: HL7423 with the logo of the 2002 FIFA World Cup emblazoned on its rear fuselage. The 2002 World Cup is scheduled to be mounted by South Korea and Japan. *Gerry Manning*

BELOW: HL7413 was Asiana's first 747-48E and is captured by Boeing's photographer lifting off from Everett. Delivery was 1 November 1991. *Boeing*

BRITISH AIRWAYS

British Airways is one of the most influential operators of the 747, having begun its association with the aircraft (as BOAC) in 1970. Since that time, the 747 has formed the backbone of BA's long-range fleet, and total new aircraft orders over the years have exceeded 100. The current fleet includes 31 'Classic' 200 series, and 39 747-400s: a further 27 -400s are due for delivery over the next three or four years, by which time the older three-crew fleet will have been sold off or retired.

ABOVE RIGHT: G-CIVA *City of St Davids/Dinas Tyddewi* has British Airways' original 747-400 colour scheme on the fuselage but the tail represents British Asia Airways. *Geoff Harber*

RIGHT: G-BNLM *City of Durham* with interim corporate colour scheme. *Geoff Harber*

BELOW: G-BNLP *City of Aberdeen* landing at Heathrow. *Leo Marriott*

BA's striking new colour schemes have aroused considerable interest, not all of it complimentary. Here (ABOVE, TOP and BOTTOM) two early computer-generated examples of the schemes and a view of the real thing (RIGHT) named 'Wunula Dreaming' on G-BNLS *City of Chester*. *British Airways; Robbie Shaw*

BALARINJI

BRITISH AIRWAYS

BRUNEI GOVERNMENT

In April 1992 the Government of Brunei purchased a 747-430 aircraft, which had nominally been prepared to Lufthansa's CF6-80C2-powered specification. It was first flown on 25 March 1992, carrying the Boeing test-registration N6009F: the aircraft was then delivered as D-ABVM on 17 April 1992, before being equipped for its new role and finally handed over as V8-AL1 — the registration reading as AL *one*, rather than AL *eye*.

ABOVE: Two views of 747-430 V8-AL1, a regular visitor to Heathrow. *Gerry Manning*

CANADIAN AIRLINES INTERNATIONAL

The first of four 747-475 GE CF6-80C2-powered aircraft for Canadian Airlines International, C-GMWW, was delivered just in time for the 1990 Christmas season, and the last (C-FGHZ) arrived during the late summer of 1994. No further orders have been received by Boeing.

ABOVE AND BELOW: Two views of Canadian's C-GMWW — at Kai Tak, Hong Kong (ABOVE), and taking- off from Everett carrying Boeing's test registration N6018N. Named *Maxwell Ward* it now has a fleet number of 881. Note the obscuration of the central fuselage by the mist generated by the wing. *Boeing*

CARGOLUX

The Luxembourg-based all-cargo airline, Cargolux, had already been operating a number of 747-200C convertible aircraft, before it announced the purchase of three GE-powered 747-400Fs in December 1990. These were the first pure freighter models actually delivered to a customer — with the first pair (LX-FCV and LX-GCV) arriving in Europe during November and December 1993 respectively. A fourth aircraft — originally ordered by Air France — was purchased from desert storage in September 1995, and a fifth (Cargolux ordered) was delivered in December 1997. A new contract has now been signed for five additional aircraft, but these will all be powered by the new Rolls-Royce RB211-524GH/T.

ABOVE RIGHT: LX-ICV, a 747-428F, was originally ordered by Air France as F-GIUA, but was not taken up. *M. McCalla*

RIGHT: The same aircraft is seen at Prestwick in August 1997. *Dave Malt*

BELOW: LX-GCV is a 747-4R7F seen at Manchester in June 1996. *P. E. Price*

CATHAY PACIFIC

Passenger traffic into Hong Kong has collapsed since the June 1997 handover to China, with severe effects on Cathay. Of its current fleet of 38 747s, no fewer than 25 are high-capacity 300-series (6) and 400-series (19) passenger aircraft, and two others are -400Fs acquired from Air Hong Kong. Cathay was launch customer for the Rolls-Royce powered 747-400, with the first delivery (VR-HOP) arriving in Hong Kong on 8 June 1989.

ABOVE: 747-467 VR-HUG (now B-HUG) seen in June 1997; since the takeover of Hong Kong by the Chinese, all Cathay serials have become Bs. *Gerry Manning*

ABOVE RIGHT: VR-HOT in the new Cathay colour scheme. *Gerry Manning*

RIGHT: VR-HOP at Manchester on a soggy 10 September 1995. *M. McCalla*

CHINA AIRLINES

At the end of December 1997, China Airlines was still operating six of its seven 747-400s, having managed to write-off B-165 while attempting to land at Kai Tak, in November 1993 (this is still the only total loss of a 747-400 anywhere in the world). The first of five aircraft (B-161) was delivered to China Airlines in February 1990, and the last (the luckless B-165) arrived in September 1993 — just two months before the accident. A second batch of five has been ordered, and at the time of writing only two of these had actually reached Taipei.

Mandarin Airlines

Wholly owned by China Airlines, Mandarin started operations with a pair of 747SPs leased from its parent. Its sole 747-400 (B-16801) was delivered during May 1995. It shares the same 09 Boeing customer-code number as all the China Airlines fleet.

Left: B-164, its wing heavy with fuel, taxiing out for departure from Los Angeles. *Leo Marriott*

Below Left: The first China Airlines 747-409, B-161, departing a damp Everett on its delivery trip, 8 February 1990. *Boeing*

Above and Below: Two views of 747-458 4X-ELB seen on 5 May 1997; it was delivered to the airline in May 1994. *Hugh Newell*

EL AL ISRAEL AIRLINES

The Israeli flag-carrier operates a total of 13 747s, but only three of them are 747-400s. The first of these (4X-ELA) was delivered on 27 April 1994, followed exactly a month later by 4X-ELB: the third and final aircraft (4X-ELC) arrived on 31 May 1995. There have been no additional orders.

EVA Airways

Beginning scheduled services only in 1991, EVA Airways is now one of the fastest-growing airlines in the world. Between November 1992 and January 1998 no fewer than 13 747-400s were delivered to its Taipei headquarters, four of them Combis. Of the 13 aircraft nominally on its books, six (including all the Combi models) are leased from various banks and financial institutions: these all carry full EVA colours, but American civil registrations. The other seven are all owned by the new airline and carry Taiwanese registrations. The first to be delivered was B-16401, which reached Taipei on 2 November 1992.

ABOVE RIGHT AND BELOW: Two views of B-14601 seen at Los Angeles. *Geoff Harber*

RIGHT: 747-45E N405EV was delivered to EVA on 15 June 1993. *Gerry Manning*

GARUDA INDONESIA AIRWAYS

State-owned Garuda operates a mixed fleet of 747s, including the 200 series, a 200 Combi and three -400s. Two more 747-400s are on order.

ABOVE: The first 400-series delivery (PK-GSG) was made to Garuda on 14 January 1994. This is PK-GSH, a 747-4U3 delivered in May 1994.

BELOW: 747-441 PK-GSI at Schiphol in August 1997. Delivered to ILFC/Varig in June 1992, Garuda leased it on 26 March 1995. *Gerry Manning*

JAPAN AIRLINES

Like so many airlines in Asia, Japan Airlines has been forced to confront big losses over the last few years, and this may influence its future fleet acquisitions. It currently operates a combined fleet of 37 747-400s and 747-400Ds, in addition to more than 40 'Classic' three-crew aircraft of almost every description — making it the world's biggest fleet of 747s. Five additional -400s are scheduled for 1998 delivery, accompanied by the planned retirement of at least seven of the older aircraft during the next two years. In an attempt to stem further losses, the JAL workforce has been reduced from about 22,000 in 1994 to less than 17,000 at the end of 1997. One bright spot in JAL's overall performance has been an increasingly large share of the domestic market.

ABOVE LEFT: 20-1101 of the Japanese Self Defense Forces at Gatwick. *Robbie Shaw*

LEFT and BELOW LEFT: JA8088 landing at Heathrow. Note the blanked off windows around the passenger door immediately aft of the wing: the variety of passenger cabin configurations means that galley positions are individual customer options. *Geoff Harber*

ABOVE: PH-BFT *City of Tokyo,* a 747-406 Combi, seen at KLM's home airport of Schiphol. It was delivered to the airline on 15 May 1997. *Gerry Manning*

BELOW: PH-BFC *City of Calgary,* in KLM Asia colours at Schiphol in August 1997. *Gerry Manning*

JAPANESE GOVERNMENT

The two 747-47C VIP transports ordered by the Japanese Government were delivered with civilian registrations. The first (JA8091) arrived in September 1991, and the second (JA8092) followed in November that year. At the beginning of April 1992 they were transferred into the Japanese Air Force as 20-1101 and 20-1102 respectively, joining a newly formed Special Transport Squadron, the 701st Tokubetsu Yuso Kokutai.

KLM

One of the most profitable airlines in Europe, KLM has a strong working relationship with US carrier Northwest — with the two airlines offering joint transatlantic services to 12 destinations in the USA. The Dutch airline operates a mixed fleet of 747s, including -300s, -300 Combis, -400s and -400 Combis. The first conventional passenger-carrying version of the -400 (PH-BFA) was delivered on 18 May 1989, and the first Combi (PH-BFC) on 1 September 1989: all the 400-series are powered by General Electric CF6-80C2 engines.

KUWAIT AIRWAYS

Kuwait Airways has been operating a small number of 747-200B Combis since 1978, but did not acquire a two-crew digital aircraft until the end of 1994. A single CF6-80-powered example was ordered in April 1992, and 9K-ADE was delivered on 29 November 1994.

KOREAN AIRLINES

Losses for the South Korean flag-carrier amounted to more than 210 billion won in 1996, and the final 1997 results are expected to be even worse. This might have a significant effect on KAL's ability to accept on-time delivery of its six remaining 747 orders (at the end of December 1997), and 10 outstanding 777s. The airline currently has 24 747-400 passenger models in service; one 747 Combi, and two 747-400F dedicated cargo aircraft. The first 400 series delivery to KAL was HL7477, which arrived at Seoul on 14 June 1989.

TOP LEFT: Kuwait Airways 747-469 9K-ADE at Gatwick. *Robbie Shaw*

ABOVE LEFT: Seen in June 1997, HL7486 over France. *Geoff Manning*

LEFT: Boeing publicity shot of the first Korean 747-4B5 and the ninth 747-400, HL7477 which was delivered in June 1989. *Boeing*

TOP: D-ABVN *Dortmund* delivered in May 1992 and seen in June 1997. *Gerry Manning*

ABOVE: 747-430 Combi D-ABTD is seen in Condor Flugdienst colours in March 1995 at Bangkok. *Gerry Manning*

LUFTHANSA

Lead customer for CF6-80 engines on the 747-400, the first aircraft (D-ABVB) flew first on 27 June 1988, although sister ship (D-ABVA) became the first -400 in Europe, delivered on 23 May 1989. Since then, 15 new passenger models and six Combis have been delivered to Lufthansa, all of them powered by GE CF6-80C2 engines. Most are named after German cities. A new order for five -400s was confirmed in early January, with 2000 and 2002 delivery dates.

Condor Flugdienst

Condor is a Munich-based airline, a wholly-owned subsidiary of Lufthansa since take-over in 1960, flying mainly to tourist destinations under various charter arrangements. At least two 747-400s have nominally been purchased in Condor's name (as seen above) — and indeed have been operated in Condor livery — but the aircraft always carry Boeing's 747-430 (Lufthansa) customer-number, and generally spend most of their operating lives with the parent company.

MALAYSIA AIRLINES

MAS is under considerable government pressure to reduce spending, which may result in cancellation or deferral of nine outstanding 747-400 orders, and up to 11 Rolls-Royce powered 777s. MAS has recently sold two of its early CF6-80-powered 747-400 Combis to a new start-up carrier, Fiji International Airlines. The idea behind this move is to standardise on its later choice of PW4000 power. At the present time MAS appears to be operating up to 13 747-400s, but its fleet plans are necessarily fluid.

ABOVE: 9M-MPB, a 747-4H6 named *Shah Alam*, seen over Heathrow, March 1997. *Hugh Newell*

ABOVE RIGHT: 9M-MPG *Kuala Trengganu* seen landing at Heathrow during June 1995, three months after its delivery to the airline. *Gerry Manning*

RIGHT: 9M-MPH *Langkawi* was delivered in September 1994. *Geoff Harber*

NORTHWEST AIRLINES

Northwest Orient Airlines (later Northwest) became the launch customer for the 747-400 when it ordered 10 standard passenger aircraft in October 1985. The first (N663US) was delivered on 26 January 1989 — some six week later than originally planned — and the last arrived just 19 months later. All ten of the original aircraft remain in service, together with more than 30 of the earlier three-crew models. Northwest has recently ordered another four aircraft.

ABOVE AND BELOW: N669US and N667US, both seen at Schiphol in August 1997. Both were delivered in 1990 and both carry over the rear passenger door a commemorative logo reading '50 years bridging the Pacific'. *Gerry Manning*

PHILIPPINE AIRLINES

The first 747-400 for Philippine Airlines (N751PR) was delivered on 19 November 1993, and since then another three have been added to the fleet. The airline has seven outstanding 747 orders at the end of 1997, and reports suggest that four of these (planned for 1999 delivery) either have been — or soon will be — cancelled.

QANTAS

With some of the longest regular airline routes in the world Qantas has always been in the forefront of the effort to persuade Boeing to increase the maximum take-off weights and fuel capacity of the 747. With extended direct routes such as those between Los Angeles and Sydney, and Singapore–London, take-off performance is often downgraded by summer 'hot and high' temperatures. Qantas was certainly instrumental in pushing the 747-400's weight limit to 875,000lb (397,000kg), and now wants to go even higher to enable more fuel to be carried without sacrificing payload — ie passengers. The airline operates a varied fleet of 747s, including two SPs; a number of -200s, -200 Combis and -300s; and a current total of 18 -400s.

ABOVE LEFT: 747-4F6 N752PR was delivered to Philippine Airlines on 21 December 1993. It is seen here at Kai Tak. *Robbie Shaw*

LEFT: VH-OJR was delivered in October 1992. The colourful logo near the cockpit window advertises the Sydney 2000 Olympic Games. *Gerry Manning*

BELOW LEFT: Another view of VH-OJM, here seen at Manchester in August 1994. *M. McCalla*

ABOVE: 747-428 CN-RGA, ex-Air France F-OGTG, was sold to Royal Air Maroc and delivered on 4 October 1993 having been stored in the Arizona desert for several months. Photographed in June 1997 at Charles de Gaulle airport, note the unusual tractor arrangement where the nosewheel is housed inside the tractor for towing. *P. E. Price*

BELOW: VH-OJM *City Of Gosford*, a 747-438, was delivered in September 1991. *Geoff Harber*

ROYAL AIR MAROC

Morocco's predominantly government-owned airline purchased a single ex-Air France 747-428 in October 1993, after the aircraft had spent some time in storage at Marana, in Arizona. It now carries the registration CN-RGA.

SAUDI ARABIAN AIRLINES

Saudi Arabian Airlines is the largest carrier in the Middle East, and has a varied fleet of modern jets. It ordered five 747-468s (the airline's first) on 18 June 1995; the first of these (HZ-AIW) was officially handed over on 22 December 1997; the others — HZ-AIV/AIX/AIY and AIZ are due for delivery up to 2001.

SINGAPORE AIRLINES

One of the largest operators of 747s in the world, SIA still has five 747-300s (of which two are Combis). Its major fleet, however, consists of 37 PW4056-powered 747-400 all-passenger models, and six 747-400F dedicated cargo aircraft. At the end of December 1997 there were outstanding orders for an additional eight passenger and two cargo aircraft.

ABOVE: Singapore Airlines 9V-SMU was the 1,000th Boeing 747 and was delivered to the airline in October 1993. It is seen at Kai Tak. *Robbie Shaw*

ABOVE RIGHT: Aerial view of 9V-SFB, a 747-412F which was delivered in September 1994. *Leo Marriott*

RIGHT: 9V-SMS, photographed 8 May 1996, was delivered in June 1993. The satellite communications aerial is the blob behind the wing on the top of the fuselage. *Geoff Harber*

SOUTH AFRICAN AIRWAYS

SAA is currently state-owned, but is soon to be privatised. It has a varied fleet of 747s, including such comparative rarities as SPs and -300s. The first of its four RR-powered 400-series (ZS-SAV) was delivered in December 1990, and the last (ZS-SAY) arrived in September 1993. The airline has recently firmed-up a commitment for yet another, which is due for delivery in 1998.

TOP: 747-444 ZS-SAX *Kempton Park* was delivered in October 1992 and is seen at Heathrow in July 1993. *Robbie Shaw*

ABOVE: ZS-SAY, a Rolls-Royce-powered 747-444 named *Vulindlela*, in June 1995. This aircraft suffered a catastrophic engine failure immediately after departing Kennedy airport for Johannesburg on 5 September 1996. (See next chapter.) *Gerry Manning*

THAI AIRWAYS INTERNATIONAL

At the end of December 1997, the Thai Airways 747 fleet consisted of one 200-series freighter, two 300-series passenger aircraft, and 12 out of a total order for 14 747-400s: the two outstanding aircraft are scheduled for 1998 delivery. The first two of Thai's 747-400s (HS-TGH and HS-TGJ) arrived in Bangkok during February and March 1990.

ABOVE: 747-4D7 HS-TGP was delivered in November 1994. It is seen here on take-off from Heathrow. *Geoff Harber*

BELOW: HS-TGJ *Hariphunchai* seen in June 1997 at Frankfurt; it was delivered in March 1990. *Gerry Manning*

UNITED AIRLINES

The huge United Airlines organisation already has nearly 30 PW400-powered 747-400s in service, with another 20 still to come over the next few years. The initial orders amounted to 15 aircraft, with further batches following as Pacific traffic increased and older fleets of aircraft were replaced. The first deliveries to United (N171UA and N172UA) were made on 25 May and 20 June 1989. United became the first company to offer -400 flights from the US to Australia and Hong Kong. In October 1996 it launched the longest non-stop scheduled service in the world with the 7,789-mile 16hr Chicago-Hong Kong route.

BELOW: United's N191UA at Kai Tak, Hong Kong. *Robbie Shaw*

BOTTOM: N187UA, a 747-422, was delivered to United in March 1993, and sports UA's new colour scheme. *Geoff Harber*

VARIG

Varig operated a trio of 747-400s (PP-VPG, H and I) for varying periods between 1991 and 1994, alongside its own fleet of three-crew passenger and Combi versions of the 747-300. The two-crew aircraft were all leased from ILFC, and when they became entangled in the wild fluctuations of the Brazilian economy, they were returned to America and the arrangement was never renewed.

TOP: A United 747-222 over Kai Tak. Note old colour scheme. *Robbie Shaw*

ABOVE: PP-VPI, a 747-475 originally destined for Canadian Airlines International and not taken up, was leased to Varig for for three years in the early 1990s before going to Air New Zealand. It is seen here over Heathrow in August 1992. *Robbie Shaw*

VIRGIN ATLANTIC

Richard Branson's Virgin Group has managed to escape from the stuffy image of big business, without becoming too trivial and so not taken seriously. An example of this philosophy has been the brilliantly original combination of names and registrations given to Virgin Atlantic's aircraft. The first 747-400 arrived in April 1994, and was christened *Lady Penelope* — after TV's 'Thunderbirds' character — to match the previously reserved registration G-VFAB. Mike Oldfield's early success with Branson (which in a way laid the foundation-stone of the whole business empire) was fondly remembered when G-VHOT became *Tubular Belle.* Others with musical connections are *Virginia Plain* (G-VTOP) and *Ruby Tuesday* (on order). Others have allied small names with big registrations — so *Tinker Belle* for G-VBIG and *Ladybird* for G-VAST.

ABOVE: Virgin Atlantic's G-VHOT *Tubular Belle,* with Scarlet Lady sporting a Virgin flag, seen in May 1997. Compare this picture with that at right. *Rob Holder*

ABOVE RIGHT: 747-4Q8 G-VFAB *Lady Penelope,* named after Gerry Anderson's 'Thunderbirds' TV programme puppet character, seen in July 1997. *Geoff Harber*

RIGHT: As a further dig against British Airways and the decision to replace the Union Flag in its new colour schemes, Richard Branson changed the Scarlet Lady's flag accordingly. It is seen on G-VTOP *Virginia Plain. Virgin*

7 ACCIDENTS & INCIDENTS

The following is a brief summary of all the known accidents and incidents involving 747-400s. Most of them are British owned or British-engined aircraft — not because they are inherently less reliable than any of the others, but simply because the information is more readily available on this side of the Atlantic.

10 October 1990: G-BNLC   Bangkok

This British Airways aircraft was carrying 238 passengers and 17 crew when it suffered a brake-overheat warning and subsequent fire shortly after touchdown at Bangkok. A full emergency evacuation was successfully carried out, and there were no injuries to any of the occupants. The fire was quickly dealt with, and damage was not extensive.

30 October 1990: G-BNLJ   Bangkok

This second British Airways incident might have happened anywhere en route, but it was actually discovered at Bangkok during a turn-round inspection. It was found that a section of wing leading-edge inboard of the No.2 engine had detached and fallen away.

Nothing was noticed during the inbound flight, and a search of the airport failed to find the missing section. The aircraft was quickly repaired and returned to service.

19 September 1991: N663US   In flight, near Tokyo

This Northwest Airlines aircraft was climbing to cruise altitude after a normal take-off from Tokyo, when a fire developed inside the No.2 engine pylon. The incident was later traced to a faulty electrical cable that had been chafing on a fuel-pipe union: this eventually began to arc onto the pipe, which quickly burned through and released fuel into the pylon. The fire occurred some distance from the engine-fire sensors, with the result that the pilots had no real warning of what was going on. Heat began to effect pipes and cables passing through the leading-edge of the wing, generating false EICAS warnings of thrust-reverser deployment and an impending stall: the bleed-air delivery duct from No.1 engine overheated, and the cabin pressurisation system eventually failed. The aircraft returned to Tokyo for a full emergency landing, and 30 passengers were injured during the subsequent evacuation.

12 April 1992: N182UA   San Francisco

Carrying 349 passengers and 20 crew, this United Airlines aircraft had just started to accelerate on the runway when an auxiliary power unit (APU) failure caused large quantities of smoke to enter the passenger cabin. The take-off was aban-

doned and 11 passengers were injured during the subsequent evacuation.

9 May 1993: JA8096   Tokyo

This All Nippon 747-400D 'domestic' aircraft was on the ground at Tokyo Narita when oil smoke from a faulty APU found its way into the cabin via the air-conditioning system. Eight of the 475 passengers were hurt, but it is not clear whether they were overcome by smoke or injured during an evacuation.

12 September 1993: F-GITA   Tahiti

Shortly after a night touchdown at Papeeta, this Air France aircraft slewed off the runway and came to a halt with its nose and inboard engines semi-submerged in a shallow lagoon. All the passengers and crew escaped without injury. The pilot later reported problems with the engine-control (Fadec) system of the General Electric CF6-80C2-powered aircraft. The aircraft left the runway to the right, and when it was later inspected it was discovered that No.1 (port outer) engine did not have its thrust-reverser deployed.

16 October 1993: 9V-???   In flight, near Bucharest

This (unknown) Singapore Airlines aircraft appears to have lost airspeed and stalled while at cruising altitude on a normal Singapore to Heathrow service: witnesses in the cabin reported buffeting and audible stall-warnings, before some of the cabin staff were thrown off their feet and passengers drinks hit the ceiling. The pilots later said that one of the airspeed indicators appeared to be displaying 'frozen' readings, and was therefore disagreeing with the other: the incident occurred while they were considering which instrument was providing the correct information. Boeing (and its suppliers) examined all the equipment, systems and software that might have had a bearing on the problem, but found nothing wrong. The aircraft itself was undamaged, and after a thorough check was returned to service.

4 November 1993: B-165   Hong Kong

Inbound from Taipei, Taiwan, this almost-new China Airlines aircraft arrived at Hong Kong's Kai Tak airport during a severe tropical storm. In squally rain and windshear conditions, the pilots appeared to touch-down some distance beyond the threshold and overran the runway — coming to rest slightly tail-down in the shallow harbour. All 269 people on board survived, but the aircraft itself was extensively damaged, and later written-off as a result of water contamination and ovoid distortion of the main fuselage frames. The $145 million hull was sold by its insurers to Hong Kong Aircraft Engineering Company (HAECO) for less than $200,000. The aircraft was later dismantled and parts of it were salvaged — with the cockpit section now being used as an instrument training aid at Xiamen, in China. At the time of writing (March 1998) this was the only recorded total loss of a 747-400 hull.

25 November 1993: VR-???   **In flight, near Los Angeles**
This (unidentified) Cathay Pacific aircraft was climbing through 21,000ft, having just departed Los Angeles bound for Hong Kong, when it suffered a fan-blade separation from one of its RB211524H engines - the first such failure in more than 12-million engine hours. The failure was fully contained, but it caused vibration severe enough to warrant a thorough structural check of the pylon and engine-mounting pins. After examining the complete engine back at Derby, Rolls-Royce was unable to discover a reason for the separation, which occurred about 30mm from the blade root: there was no obvious manufacturing fault, and no signs of subsequent external damage.

10 November 1994: G-BNLA   **In flight, near Buenos Aires**
The crew of this British Airways aircraft shut down the No.4 engine after what were described as 'a series of loud bangs', followed by a rise in exhaust gas temperature and an engine fire warning. The incident occurred soon after take-off, and the aircraft returned safely to Buenos Aires. Subsequent examination of the engine revealed that part of the combustion chamber had cracked, and been displaced, changing the flow path of some of the hot gases This 'blow-torch' effect had managed to burn through the engine inner-casing, and then through the outer casing of the engine core. Later action by Rolls-Royce included a change of materials specification for the combustion chamber lining, and a rolling modification programme as each engine came up for its major overhaul

17 Feb 95: N751PR   **Honolulu**
The No.1 engine of this Philippine Airlines aircraft was hit and damaged by a low-loader truck The truck was on a parallel taxiway at night, and the driver failed to realize that the inbound flight would be turning in towards its stand. The damage was not serious, there was no fire and none of the 398 occupants were hurt.

17 Mar 95: G-BNLA   **Heathrow**
This aircraft was the innocent victim of a ground collision between two British Airways 747s. A 747-200 (G-BDXA) was under tow, with nosewheel steering and most of the braking effort being provided by the tractor. A strong gust of wind rocked the aircraft, snapping the tow-bar and breaking the electrical connection between the tractor and the aircraft systems. The on-board brakeman initially managed to stop the aircraft, but without a continuing supply of hydraulic power he was unable to prevent it moving again. The strong wind and sloping ground caused it to gradually accelerate into the stationary 747-400, causing substantial damage to both aircraft.

28 May 95: VR-HOX   **Hong Kong**
Carrying 398 passengers and 21 crew this Cathay Pacific aircraft had just taken-off from Kai Tak Airport when the No.2 engine (port inner) suffered an internal failure and caught fire. The fire was extinguished and the aircraft returned for a safe emergency landing, but 21 people were hurt during the subsequent evacuation.

30 May 96: G-VHOT   **Iqualuit, Canada**
During a scheduled transatlantic flight, one of the passengers on this Virgin Atlantic aircraft developed a life-threatening illness, and the captain diverted to Iqualuit, in the North West Territories. While taxying under the guidance of three marshallers, the No.4 engine (starboard outer) struck the airport's small refuelling station and sustained major damage.

5 Sep 96: F-GITF   **In flight, over Burkina Faso**
While at cruising altitude on a normal scheduled flight, this Air France aircraft encountered severe turbulence associated with a powerful weather front. Three passengers were seriously hurt, and one of them subsequently died from injuries caused by hitting an in-flight entertainment system screen.

5 Sep 96: ZS-SAY   **On take-off, New York**
This South African Airways aircraft suffered an engine failure at about 750ft, immediately after departure from Kennedy Airport, bound for Johannesburg. The engine concerned was an RB211-524H, which was fitted with the original '2b-standard' directionally-solidified high-pressure turbine-blades (see main text). One of the blades in No.3 engine failed, causing it to be shut down, and a subsequent inspection revealed that a similar blade in the same aircraft's No.1 engine was also on the point of failure.

5 Apr 97: G-BNLF   **Malawi**
This British Airways aircraft suffered significant damage while attempting to land at Lilongwe Airport, Malawi, during a heavy rainstorm; the GPWS sounded a 'sink-rate' alarm immediately before touchdown, and windshear may have played a part in the subsequent 2.85g initial impact. The aircraft bounced into the air again after this first contact, and the crew initiated a go around, which was followed by a perfectly normal landing. After a full 'heavy-landing' inspection at Lilongwe, the aircraft was returned to service and flew two more sectors before finally arriving at Gatwick: only at Gatwick was the extent of the damage fully realized, and the aircraft withdrawn from service. After being ferried to BA's maintenance headquarters at Heathrow a thorough check revealed a frightening degree of damage. The repairs took six weeks to complete and cost several million pounds.

8 PRODUCTION LIST

The details below represent all 747-400 aircraft manufactured at Everett between April 1988 and January 1998. Boeing construction numbers are allotted at the time of contract signature, and bear little relationship to the order of manufacture: the aircraft are therefore listed in factory line number order. The last two digits of the model number represent the Boeing customer code number (the source of the original airframe order and therefore its general specification): a small number of these contracts were later taken over by other airlines, so the customer code does not always coincide with the name of the first operator. Many of these aircraft were first flown carrying one of the special US test registrations allocated to Boeing, but they are shown here with original delivery registrations and original airline purchasers.

Line	c/n	Model	Airline	Registration	First Flight
696	23719	451	Northwest Airlines	N661US	29 Apr 88
700	23817	430	Lufthansa	D-ABVB	27 Jun 88
705	23814	467	Cathay Pacific	VR-HOO	28 Aug 88
708	23720	451	Northwest Airlines	N662US	21 Sep 88
711	24159	437	Air India	VT-EPW	26 Sep 88
715	23818	451	Northwest Airlines	N663US	8 Dec 88
717	24061	412	Singapore Airlines	9V-SMA	15 Mar 98
719	24160	437	Air India	VT-EPX	8 Nov 88
721	23819	451	Northwest Airlines	N664US	4 Apr 89
722	24062	412	Singapore Airlines	9V-SMB	6 Feb 89
723	23816	430	Lufthansa	D-ABVA	21 Apr 89
725	23999	406	KLM	PH-BFA	15 Apr 89
726	23820	451	Northwest Airlines	N665US	27 Jul 89
727	23908	436	British Airways	G-BNLA	3 Jun 89
728	23815	467	Cathay Pacific	VR-HOP	2 May 89
729	24198	4B5	Korean Air	HL7477	13 May 89
730	23909	436	British Airways	G-BNLB	7 Jul 89
731	24354	438	Qantas	VH-OJA	3 Jul 89
732	24000	406	KLM	PH-BFB	23 May 89
733	24322	422	United Airlines	N171UA	25 May 89

BA 747-436 G-BNLT over Heathrow. *Gerry Manning*

Line	c/n	Model	Airline	Registration	First Flight
734	23910	436	British Airways	G-BNLC	28 Jun 89
735	23982	406 Combi	KLM	PH-BFC	30 Jun 89
736	24063	412	Singapore Airlines	9V-SMC	21 Jun 89
737	24001	406 Combi	KLM	PH-BFD	24 Aug 89
738	24315	4H6 Combi	Malaysia Airlines	9M-MHL	1 Oct 89
739	24199	4B5	Korean Air	HL7478	15 Jul 89
740	24363	422	United Airlines	N172UA	20 Jul 89
741	24154	4B3	UTA	F-GEXA	1 Aug 89
742	23821	451	Northwest Airlines	N666US	31 Jul 89
743	24346	4J6 Combi	Air China	B-2456	10 Sep 89
744	23911	436	British Airways	G-BNLD	16 Aug 89
745	24405	4H6 Combi	Malaysia Airlines	9M-MHM	8 Sep 89
806	24382	422	United Airlines	N175UA	7 Aug 90
807	24806	438	Qantas	VH-OJH	14 Aug 90
808	24836	4H6	Malaysia Airlines	9M-MHN	20 Aug 90
809	24226	412	Singapore Airlines	9V-SMG	23 Aug 90
811	24383	422	United Airlines	N176UA	31 Aug 90
812	24833	481	All Nippon	JA8095	13 Sep 90
813	24851	467	Cathay Pacific	VR-HOT	18 Sep 90
815	24855	419	Air New Zealand	ZK-NBT	28 Sep 90
816	24730	47C	Japanese Gov't VIP	JA8091	9 Oct 90
817	24057	436	British Airways	G-BNLO	9 Oct 90
819	24384	422	United Airlines	N177UA	19 Oct 90
820	24385	422	United Airlines	N178UA	23 Oct 90
821	24870	446	Japan Airlines	JA8078	29 Oct 90
823	24883	475	Canadian AL Int	C-GMWW	6 Nov 90
824	24885	446	Japan Airlines	JA8079	13 Nov 90
825	24886	446	Japan Airlines	JA8080	20 Nov 90
826	24887	438	Qantas	ZS-SAV	27 Nov 90
827	24976	444	South African AW	VH-OJI	3 Dec 90
828	24058	436	British Airways	G-BNLP	4 Dec 90
829	24447	436	British Airways	G-BNLR	11 Dec 90
830	24621	4B5	Korean Air	HL7481	14 Dec 90
831	24227	412	Singapore Airlines	9VSMH	3 Jan 91
832	24920	481	All Nippon	JA8096	4 Jan 91
833	24993	4D7	Thai Airways Int	HS-TGK	11 Jan 91
834	24925	467	Cathay Pacific	VR-HOU	10 Jan 91
835	24974	438	Qantas	VH-OJJ	18 Jan 91
836	24969	428	Air France	F-GITA	25 Jan 91
837	24895	475	Canadian AL Int	C-FCRA	30 Jan 91
838	24975	412	Singapore Airlines	9V-SMI	5 Feb 91
839	24731	47C	Japanese Gov't VIP	JA8092	8 Feb 91
840	24998	433 Combi	Air Canada	C-GAGL	15 Feb 91
841	24629	436	British Airways	G-BNLS	20 Feb 91
842	24630	436	British Airways	G-BNLT	26 Feb 91
843	24990	428 Combi	Air France	F-GITB	28 Feb 91
844	25213	446D	Japan Airlines	JA8083	15 Mar 91
845	25045	430	Lufthansa	D-ABVH	14 Mar 91
846	24966	430 Combi	Lufthansa	D-ABTE	20 Mar 91
847	25046	430	Lufthansa	D-ABVK	26 Mar 91
848	24967	430 Combi	Lufthansa	D-ABTF	29 Mar 91
849	25082	467	Cathay Pacific	VR-HOV	5 Apr 91
850	25086	406	KLM	PH-BFI	11 Apr 91

Line	c/n	Model	Airline	Registration	First Flight
851	25064	446	Japan Airlines	JA8081	17 Apr 91
852	25068	412	Singapore Airlines	9VSMJ	23 Apr 91
853	25205	4B5	Korean Air	HL7482	29 Apr 91
854	25087	406	KLM	PH-BFK	3 May 91
855	24896	475	Varig	PP-VPI	8 May 91
856	25047	430	Lufthansa	D-ABTH	15 May 91
857	25067	438	Qantas	VH-OJK	21 May 91
858	25126	4H6	Malaysia Airlines	9M-MHO	29 May 91
859	25127	412	Singapore Airlines	9V-SMK	4 Jun 91
860	25128	412	Singapore Airlines	9V-SML	6 Jun 91
861	25152	444	South African AW	ZS-SAW	13 Jun 91
862	25074	433 Combi	Air Canada	C-GAGM	19 Jun 91
863	25135	481	All Nippon	JA8097	25 Jun 91
864	24155	4B3 Combi	UTA	F-GEXB	28 Jun 91
865	25151	438	Qantas	VH-OJL	5 Jul 91
866	25158	422	United Airlines	N179UA	11 Jul 91
867	25224	422	United Airlines	N180UA	17 Jul 91
868	25075	433 Combi	Air Canada	C-GAGN	24 Jul 91
869	24311	409	China Airlines	B-163	26 Jul 91
870	25207	481	All Nippon	JA8098	2 Aug 91
871	25212	446	Japan Airlines	JA8082	8 Aug 91
872	25238	428 Combi	Air France	F-GISA	14 Aug 91
873	25211	467	Cathay Pacific	VR-HOW	13 Aug 91
874	25275	4B5	Korean Air	HL7483	26 Aug 91
875	25245	438	Qantas	VH-OJM	30 Aug 91
876	25260	446	Japan Airlines	JA8085	6 Sep 91
877	24955	467	Cathay Pacific	VR-HOX	11 Sep 91

Virgin Atlantic 747-4Q8 G-VFAB Lady Penelope. Leo Marriott

Line	c/n	Model	Airline	Registration	First Flight
878	25266	228F	Air France	F-GCBN	19 Sep 91
879	25214	446D	Japan Airlines	JA8084	25 Sep 91
880	25405	48E	Asiana Airlines	HL7413	27 Sep 91
881	25278	422	United Airlines	N181UA	3 Oct 91
882	25279	422	United Airlines	N182UA	8 Oct 91
883	25317	438	Qantas	VH-OJN	15 Oct 91
884	25302	428 Combi	Air France	F-GISB	21 Oct 91
885	25308	446	Japan Airlines	JA8086	25 Oct 91
886	25171	281F	Nippon Cargo AL	JA8194	4 Nov 91
887	25351	467	Cathay Pacific	VR-HOY	7 Nov 91
888	25356	406	KLM	PH-BFL	12 Nov 91
889	25344	428	Air France	F-GITC	15 Nov 91
890	25366	4D7	Thai Airways Int	HS-TGL	22 Nov 91
891	25292	481D	All Nippon	JA8099	27 Nov 91
892	25452	48E	Asiana Airlines	HL7414	5 Dec 91
893	26392	4B5	Korean Air	HL7484	11 Dec 91
894	25544	438	Qantas	VH-OJO	21 Feb 92
895	25406	436	British Airways	G-BNLU	20 Dec 91
896	26373	406	KLM	PH-BFN	8 Jan 92
897	26346	446	Japan Airlines	JA8087	14 Jan 92
898	26425	430	Lufthansa	D-ABVL	20 Jan 92
899	25599	428 Combi	Air France	F-GISC	23 Jan 92
900	25427	436	British Airways	G-BNLV	30 Jan 92
901	25600	428	Air France	F-GITD	5 Feb 92
902	26341	446	Japan Airlines	JA8088	11 Feb 92
903	25432	436	British Airways	G-BNLW	17 Feb 92
904	25879	4J6	Air China	B-2464	1 Feb 92

KLM 747-406 Combi PH-BFC at Schiphol. *Dave Malt*

Line	c/n	Model	Airline	Registration	First Flight
905	26342	446	Japan Airlines	JA8089	7 Feb 92
906	25601	428	Air France	F-GITE	4 Mar 92
907	26347	446D	Japan Airlines	JA8090	6 Mar 92
908	25435	436	British Airways	G-BNLX	16 Mar 92
909	25602	428	Air France	F-GITF	20 Nov 92
910	26426	430	Lufthansa	D-ABVM	25 Mar 92
911	25379	422	United Airlines	N183UA	1 Apr 92
912	25422	475	Canadian AL Int	C-FBCA	7 Apr 92
913	25380	422	United Airlines	N184UA	13 Apr 92
914	25639	481D	All Nippon	JA8955	14 Apr 92
915	26427	430	Lufthansa	D-ABVN	23 Apr 92
916	25545	438	Qantas	VH-OJP	29 Apr 92
917	24956	441	ILFC/Varig	PP-VPG	5 May 92
918	26343	446	Japan Airlines	JA8901	11 May 92
919	25395	422	United Airlines	N185UA	15 May 92
920	25640	481D	All Nippon	JA8955	21 May 92
921	26547	412	Singapore Airlines	9V-SMM	22 May 92
922	26395	4B5	Korean Air	HL7485	May 92
923	26548	412	Singapore Airlines	9V-SMN	5 Jun 92
924	25546	438	Qantas	VH-OJQ	15 Jun 92
925	25871	467	Cathay Pacific	VR-HOZ	12 Jun 92
926	25880	4J6	Air China	B-2466	25 Jun 92
921	25642	481D	All Nippon	JA8957	1 Jul 92
928	25641	481	All Nippon	JA8958	21 Jul 92
929	26344	446	Japan Airlines	JA8902	23 Jul 92
930	25872	467	Cathay Pacific	VR-HUA	16 Jul 92
931	26875	422	United Airlines	N186UA	6 Aug 92
932	27042	4H6	Malaysia Airlines	9M-MPA	11 Aug 92
933	25605	419	Air New Zealand	ZK-NBU	17 Aug 92
934	25628	428	Air France	F-GISD	24 Aug 92
935	26345	446D	Japan Airlines	JA8903	28 Aug 92
936	25547	438	Qantas	VH-OJR	3 Sep 92
937	25873	467	Cathay Pacific	VR-HUB	10 Sep 92
938	25413	406 Combi	KLM	PH-BFO	16 Sep 92
939	26876	422	United Airlines	N187UA	18 Sep 92
940	27066	412	Singapore Airlines	9V-SMO	28 Sep 92
941	26348	446D	Japan Airlines	JA8904	1 Oct 92
942	27062	45E	EVA Airways	B16401	8 Oct 92
943	26637	444	South African AW	ZS-SAX	27 Oct 92
944	26877	422	United Airlines	N188UA	3 Oct 92
945	27093	4D7	Thai Airways Int	HS-TGM	23 Oct 92
946	25777	48E	Asiana Airlines	HL7415	30 Oct 92
947	27063	45E	EVA Airways	B16402	1 Nov 92
948	26349	446D	Japan Airlines	JA8905	11 Nov 92
949	25874	467	Cathay Pacific	VR-HUD	17 Nov 92
950	26615	4D7	Thai Airways Int	HS-TGN	23 Nov 92
951	26396	4B5	Korean Air	HL7486	2 Dec 92
952	25646	481D	All Nippon	JA8959	18 Dec 92
953	27067	412	Singapore Airlines	9V-SMP	12 Dec 92
954	24312	409	China Airlines	B-164	17 Dec 92
955	27132	412	Singapore Airlines	9V-SMQ	22 Dec 92
956	25629	428	Air France	F-OGTG	7 Jan 93
957	25881	4J6	Air China	B-2443	15 Jan 93

ANA 747-481 JA8094 takes-off from Everett. *Boeing*

Line	c/n	Model	Airline	Registration	First Flight
958	26393	4B5	Korean Air	HL7487	20 Jan 93
959	27090	436	British Airways	G-BNLY	25 Jan 93
960	25630	428 Combi	Air France	F-GISE	29 Jan 93
961	26350	446	Japan Airlines	JA8906	5 Feb 93
962	27133	412	Singapore Airlines	9V-SMR	12 Feb 93
963	26351	446D	Japan Airlines	JA8907	16 Feb 93
964	27091	436	British Airways	G-BNLZ	22 Feb 93
965	25699	4H6	Malaysia Airlines	9M-MPB	26 Feb 93
966	26878	422	United Airlines	N189UA	5 Mar 93
967	27092	436	British Airways	G-CIVA	10 Mar 93
968	25632	428F	* (stored) *	N6005C	4 May 93
969	26373	406	KLM	PH-BFN	23 Mar 93
970	27117	467	Cathay Pacific	VR-HUE	30 Mar 93
971	24957	441	ILFC/Varig	PP-VPH	1 Apr 93
972	25643	481D	All Nippon	JA8960	8 Apr 93
973	26879	422	United Airlines	N19OUA	12 Apr 93
974	25700	4H6	Malaysia Airlines	9M-MPC	19 Apr 93
975	25644	481D	All Nippon	JA8961	27 Apr 93
976	27141	45E	EVA Airways	N403EV	25 Apr 93
977	24313	409	China Airlines	B-165	6 May 93
978	26352	446D	Japan Airlines	JA8908	11 May 93
979	25645	481	All Nippon	JA8962	19 May 93
980	26353	446	Japan Airlines	JA8909	21 May 93
981	27134	412	Singapore Airlines	9V-SMS	25 May 93
982	27142	45E	EVA Airways	N405EV	3 Jun 93
983	25778	48E	Asiana Airlines	HL7416	9 Jun 93
984	26880	422	United Airlines	N19lUA	14 Jun 93

Air India 747-437 Combi VT-ESO *Khajuraho. Leo Marriott*

Line	c/n	Model	Airline	Registration	First Flight
985	26473	451	United Airlines	N105UA	25 Jun 93
986	26394	4B5	Korean Air	HL7488	8 Jul 93
987	27078	437	Air India	VT-ESM	2 Jul 93
988	26474	451	United Airlines	N106UA	16 Aug 93
989	26881	422	United Airlines	N192UA	14 Jul 93
990	27137	412	Singapore Airlines	9V-SMT	4 Aug 93
991	25647	481D	All Nippon	JA8963	29 Jul 93
992	26374	406	KLM	PH-BFP	13 Aug 93
993	25869	467	Cathay Pacific	VR-HUF	5 Aug 93
994	27154	45E	EVA Airways	B-16461	25 Aug 93
995	26638	444	South African AW	ZS-SAY	1 Sep 93
996	27163	481D	All Nippon	JA8964	7 Sep 93
997	25701	4H6	Malaysia Airlines	9M-MPD	10 Sep 93
998	27173	45E	EVA Airways	B-16462	20 Sep 93
999	25702	4H6	Malaysia Airlines	9M-MPE	24 Sep 93
1000	27068	412	Singapore Airlines	9V-SMU	29 Sep 93
1001	26609	4D7	Thai Airways Int	HS-TGO	7 Oct 93
1002	25866	4R7F	Cargolux	LX-FCV	30 Oct 93
1003	27164	437	Air India	VT-ESN	21 Oct 93
1004	27174	45E	EVA Airways	B-16463	25 Oct 93
1005	27261	4F6	Philippine Airlines	N751PR	31 Oct 93
1006	25779	48E	Asiana Airlines	HL7417	8 Nov 93
1007	25870	467	Cathay Pacific	VR-HUG	8 Nov 93
1008	25867	4R7F	Cargolux	LX-GCV	24 Nov 93
1009	27165	437	Air India	VT-ESO	30 Nov 93
1010	27069	412	Singapore Airlines	9V-SMV	6 Dec 93
1011	25704	4U3	Garuda Indonesia AW	PK-GSG	13 Dec 93

Cathay 747-467 VR-HOP over Kai Tak. Leo Marriott

Line	c/n	Model		Airline	Registration	First Flight
1012	27262	4F6		Philippine Airlines	N725PR	14 Dec 93
1013	27072	4B5		Korean Air	HL7489	7 Jan 94
1014	27202	406	Combi	KLM	PH-BFR	6 Jan 94
1015	27178	412		Singapore Airlines	9V-SMW	17 Jan 94
1016	26062	45E		EVA Airways	B-16465	18 Jan 94
1017	27043	4H6		Malaysia Airlines	9M-MPF	22 Jan 94
1018	25811	436		British Airways	G-CIVB	3 Feb 94
1019	27177	4B5		Korean Air	HL7490	7 Feb 94
1020	27175	467F		Cathay Pacific	VR-HUH	21 Feb 94
1021	25882	4J6		Air China	B-2445	18 Feb 94
1022	25812	436		British Airways	G-CIVC	21 Feb 94
1023	27217	412		Singapore Airlines	9V-SMY	8 Mar 94
1024	26355	446		Japan Airlines	JA8910	7 Mar 94
1025	25703	4H6		Malaysia Airlines	9M-MPF	16 Mar 94
1026	26356	446		Japan Airlines	JA8911	23 Mar 94
1027	26055	458		El Al	4X-ELA	11 Apr 94
1028	24958	4Q8		Virgin Atlantic	G-VFAB	14 Apr 94
1029	25705	4U3		Garuda Indonesia AW	PK-GSH	27 Apr 94
1030	26549	412		Singapore Airlines	9V-SMZ	4 May 94
1031	27099	446		Japan Airlines	JA8912	16 May 94
1032	26056	458		El Al	4X-ELB	18 May 94
1033	27230	467		Cathay Pacific	VR-HUI	3 Jun 94
1034	27214	437		Air India	VT-ESP	15 Jun 94
1035	25780	48E		Asiana Airlines	HL7418	23 Jun 94
1036	26563	412F		Singapore Airlines	9V-SFA	9 Jul 94
1037	27341	4B5		Korean Air	HL7491	18 Jul 94
1038	27827	4F6		Canadian AL Int	C-FGHZ	27 Jul 94

JAL 747-446 JA8081 over Heathrow. *Rob Holder*

Line	c/n	Model	Airline	Registration	First Flight
1039	27828	4F6	Philippine Airlines	N753PR	18 Aug 94
1040	26550	412	Singapore Airlines	9V-SPA	31 Aug 94
1041	27044	4H6	Malaysia Airlines	9M-MPH	8 Sep 94
1042	26561	412F	Singapore Airlines	9V-SFB	17 Sep 94
1043	26326	4Q8	Virgin Atlantic	G-VHOT	26 Sep 94
1044	25781	48E	Asiana Airlines	HL7419	13 Oct 94
1045	26551	412	Singapore Airlines	9V-SPB	12 Oct 94
1046	27338	469	Kuwait Airways	9K-ADE	28 Oct 94
1047	26610	4D7	Thai Airways Int	HS-TGP	11 Nov 94
1048	27349	436	British Airways	G-CIVD	23 Nov 94
1049	27070	412	Singapore Airlines	9V-SPC	8 Dec 94
1050	27350	436	British Airways	G-CIVE	8 Dec 94
1051	27898	45E Combi	EVA Airways	N406EV	28 Dec 94
1052	26560	412F	Singapore Airlines	9V-SFC	2 Feb 95
1053	27899	45E Combi	EVA Airways	N407EV	26 Jan 95
1054	25883	4J6	Air China	B-2447	25 Jan 95
1055	26397	4B5	Korean Air	HL7492	16 Feb 95
1056	26552	412	Singapore Airlines	9V-SPD	6 Mar 95
1057	26398	4B5	Korean Air	HL7493	11 Mar 95
1058	25814	436	British Airways	G-CIVF	22 Mar 95
1059	25815	436	British Airways	G-CIVG	6 Apr 95
1060	27436	481D	All Nippon	JA8965	16 Apr 95
1061	27595	467	Cathay Pacific	VR-HUJ	14 May 95
1062	27915	458	El Al	4X-ELC	15 May 95
1063	27965	409	Mandarin Airlines	B-16801	16 May 95
1064	25783	48E	Asiana Airlines	HL7420	14 Jun 95
1065	27503	467	Cathay Pacific	VR-HUK	29 Jun 95
1066	27442	481D	All Nippon	JA8966	18 Jul 95
1067	27662	4B5	Korean Air	HL7494	31 Jul 95
1068	27663	469	Philippine Airlines	N754PR	28 Aug 95
1069	26553	412F	Singapore Airlines	9V-SFD	20 Aug 95
1070	26554	412	Singapore Airlines	9V-SPE	28 Sep 95
1071	27723	4D7	Thai Airways Int	HS-TGR	23 Oct 95
1072	27071	412	Singapore Airlines	9V-SPF	9 Nov 95
1073	28096	4B5	Korean Air	HL7495	17 Dec 95
1074	26562	412	Singapore Airlines	9V-SPG	9 Feb 96
1075	26555	412	Singapore Airlines	9V-SPH	1 Mar 96
1076	28092	45E Combi	EVA Airways	N408EV	14 Mar 96
1077	29093	45E Combi	EVA Airways	N409EV	29 Mar 96
1078	25809	436	British Airways	G-CIVH	11 Apr 96
1079	25814	436	British Airways	G-CIVI	22 Apr 96
1080	28086	430	Lufthansa	D-ABVO	5 May 96
1081	26255	4Q8	Virgin Atlantic	G-VBIG	28 May 96
1082	28022	412	Singapore Airlines	9V-SPI	9 Jun 96
1083	26400	4B5	Korean Air	HL7496	18 Jun 96
1084	26556	412	Singapore Airlines	9V-SPJ	9 Jul 96
1085	26890	422	United Airlines	N193UA	20 Jul 96
1086	25784	48E	Asiana Airlines	HL7421	7 Aug 96
1087	26401	4B5F	Korean Air	HL7497	23 Aug 96
1088	26892	422	United Airlines	N194UA	6 Sep 96
1089	28094	437	Air India	VT-EVA	21 Sep 96
1090	28195	406	KLM	PH-BFS	3 Oct 96
1091	27672	4H6	Malaysia Airlines	9M-MPI	16 Oct 96

Line	c/n	Model	Airline	Registration	First Flight
1092	26402	4B5	Korean Air	HL7498	20 Oct 96
1093	28095	437	Air India	VT-EVB	4 Nov 96
1094	28263	412F	Singapore Airlines	9V-SFE	15 Nov 96
1095	26403	4B5	Korean Air	HL7472	18 Nov 96
1096	28367	48EF	Asiana Airlines	HL7422	12 Dec 96
1097	26616	4D7	Thai Airways Int	HS-TGT	10 Dec 96
1098	28335	4B5	Korean Air	HL7473	14 Dec 96
1099	28023	412	Singapore Airlines	9V-SPK	12 Jan 97
1100	28194	4Q8	Virgin Atlantic	G-VTOP	14 Jan 97
1101	26557	412	Singapore Airlines	9V-SPL	21 Jan 97
1102	25817	436	British Airways	GCIVJ	31 Jan 97
1103	28284	430	Lufthansa	D-ABVP	10 Feb 97
1104	25818	436	British Airways	G-CIVK	22 Feb 97
1105	28026	412F	Singapore Alrllnes	9VSFF	28 Feb 97
1106	28285	430	Lufthansa	D-ABVR	4 Mar 97
1107	26404	4B5	Korean Air	HL7460	13 Mar 97
1108	27478	436	British Airways	G-CIVL	23 Mar 97
1109	28286	430	Lufthansa	D-ABVS	4 Apr 97
1110	28287	430	Lufthansa	D-ABVT	14 Apr 97
1111	27724	4D7	Thai Airways Int	HS-TGW	19 Apr 97
1112	28459	406	KLM	PH-BFT	1 May 97
1113	26899	422	United Airlines	N195UA	8 May 97
1114	28709	409	China Airlines	B-18201	17 May 97
1115	25782	48E	Asiana Airlines	HL7423	22 May 97
1116	28700	436	British Airways	G-CIVM	? May 97
1117	28757	41R	Virgin Atlantic	G-VAST	5 Jun 97
1118	26405	4B5	Korean Air	HL7461	12 Jun 97

Air Canada 747-433 G-GAGL over Heathrow. *Geoff Harber*

Line	c/n	Model	Airline	Registration	First Flight
1119	28754	4J6 Combi	Air China	B-2467	23 Jun 97
1120	28715	422	United Airlines	N196UA	23 Jun 97
1121	26901	422	United Airlines	N197UA	9 Jul 97
1122	28339	468	Saudi Arabian Al	HZ-AIV	14 Sep 97
1123	26406	4B5F	Korean Air	HL7462	23 Jul 97
1124	28716	422	United Airlines	N198UA	5 Aug 97
1125	25868	4R7F	Cargolux	LX-KCV	13 Aug 97
1126	28717	422	United Airlines	N199UA	8 Sep 97
1127	28196	406 Combi	KLM	PH-BFU	28 Aug 97
1128	28755	4J6	Air China	B-2468	6 Sep 97
1129	28848	436	British Airways	G-CIVN	18 Sep 97
]130	28426	4H6	Malaysia Airlines	9MMPJ	5 Oct 97
113].	28551	48E	Asiana Airlines	HL7424	–
1132	28710	409	China Airlines	B-18202	12 Oct 97
1133	28282	481	All Nippon	JA401A	29 Oct 97
1134	27725	4D7	Thai Airways Int	HS-TGX	30 Oct 97
1135	28849	436	British Airways	G-CIVO	18 Nov 97
1136	28711	409	China Airlines	B-18203	17 Nov 97
1137	28712	409	China Airlines	B-18205	7 Dec 97
1138	28340	468	Saudi Arabian Al	HZ-AIW	17 Dec 97
1139	29053	4R7F	Cargolux	LX-LCV	17 Jan 98
1140	29061	45E	EVA Airways	B-16410	16 Jan 98
1141	26902	422	United Airlines	N104UA	19 Jan 98
1142	28283	481	All Nippon	JA402A	–
1143	29101	430	Lufthansa	D-ABVM	–
1144	28850	436	British Airways	G-CIVP	–
1145	29030	409	China Airlines	B-18206	–

Air France 747-428 Combi F-GISE at Kai Tak. *Robbie Shaw*

9 CHRONOLOGY

9 Feb 1969	First flight of the Boeing 747.
11 Oct 1970	First flight of the 747-200B.
30 Nov 1971	First flight of the 747-200F.
23 March 1973	First flight of the 747-200C.
31 Aug 1973	First flight of the 747-100SR.
18 Nov 1974	First flight of the 747-200 Combi.
4 July 1975	First flight of the 747SP.
5 Oct 1982	First flight of the 747-300.
May 1985	The launch programme for the 747-400 is announced by the Boeing Company.
July 1985	Engineers start planning the 747-400.
22 Oct 1985	Northwest Airlines announces the order of 10 aircraft and so becomes the launch customer.
June-July 1976	Assembly starts on the first parts of the plane.
16 May 1987	First flight of the 747-2G4B — the VC-25A Presidential aircraft.
24 Nov 1987	First flight of the 747-300SR.
26 Jan 1988	N401PW – the first completed 747-400 off the production line rolls out at the Boeing Everett factory for the first time.
29 April 1988	First flight of the 747-400.
27 June 1988	N661US breaks the maximum take-off record weight achieving 404,994kg at Moses Lake, Washington.
10 Jan 1989	The 747-400 is certified with Pratt & Whitney PW4056 engines.
26 Jan 1989	Northwest Airlines takes delivery of its first 747-400 – designated N663US.

ABOVE: Malaysia 747-4H6 9M-MPA over Heathrow. *H. A. Newell*

BELOW RIGHT: EVA Air 747-45E B-16401. *Geoff Harber*

1 Feb 1989	Northwest Airlines first passenger-paying flight from Minneapolis–Phoenix.
8 May 1989	Certified with General Electric CF6-80C2B1F engines.
18 May 1989	Delivery of first 747-400 to KLM.
8 June 1989	Certified for Rolls Royce RB211-524G engines.
17 Aug 1989	New distance record set flying London–Sydney non-stop on a delivery flight for Qantas. A distance of 17,950km in 20 hours 8 minutes.
Sept 1989	Air France becomes the launch customer for the 747-400F when it orders five freighters.
1 Sept 1989	The 747-400(SCD) is certified by the FAA for commercial service.
Feb 1990	Launch of the 747-400F (freighter) to take over from the 747-200F.
May 1990	Boeing stops manufacture of other planes and now only offers the 747-400 family of aircraft.
11 May 1990	Certified with RB211-524H engines.

15 March 1991	N60668 became the first 747-400D to fly.
10 Oct 1991	JAL took delivery of its first 747-400D – designated JA8083.
10 Oct 1991	FAA certification for commercial service.
8 March 1993	The 747-400F was rolled out for the first time, registered N6009F and delivered to Air France – the launch customer.
7 May 1993	The first flight of the 747-400F.
Sept-Oct 1993	Certification for the 747-400F by the FAA for commercial service.
17 Nov 1993	Cargolux Airlines takes delivery of the first 747-400F, registered LX-FCV.
2 Sept 1996	President of Boeing Commercial Airplane Group, Ron Woodward, announces the preliminary design and configuration studies for two new 747s, the 747-500X and 747-600X. These plans were later shelved.
Oct 1996	United Airlines launch the longest scheduled non-stop airline service in the world using 747-400 planes. The route, Chicago–Hong Kong, is 7,789 miles and takes 16 hours.
Dec 1996	Air China orders three 747-400s, an order worth US$510 million.
Dec 1996	First conversion of a 747-400D to -400 standard with added winglets and increased MTOW.

INDEX